Russell Webb, was born in a suburb on the outskirts of East London within the county of Essex. As an adult he moved away, but kept his connections with his hometown where he continues to serve the community, working as a London Firefighter.

He never planned to become an author, however, he found writing about his experiences as a child and later about the untimely death of his wife really helped with his grieving process. He hopes that his story will help and encourage others to talk about their grief and loved ones. It's okay not to be okay!

With Love

Russell Webb

x

This book is dedicated to the everlasting memory of my beautiful Wife: Sharon Lynne Webb.

And loving memories of my mum and dad and brother Steven.

To everyone who has been affected by cancer, directly or indirectly.

And finally, to all those people like myself who have lost a loved one.

Russell Webb

LOVE BEYOND LOVE

AUSTIN MACAULEY PUBLISHERS™

LONDON • CAMBRIDGE • NEW YORK • SHARJAH

A CIP catalogue record for this title is available from the British Library.

ISBN 9781398483729 (Paperback)
ISBN 9781398483736 (Hardback)
ISBN 9781398483743 (ePub e-book)

www.austinmacauley.com

First Published 2022
Austin Macauley Publishers Ltd®
1 Canada Square
Canary Wharf
London
E14 5AA

Jan Smith, who helped with the proof reading of this book and cared for Sharon by providing relaxing reflexology whist she was having chemotherapy.

Mia Webb who has helped with the design of front and back covers. Jason Webb and Angela Judge who stayed with me and gave loving care and support to Sharon and myself in her final hours.

To all my family, who continue to love and support me.

Table of Contents

Intro

LOVE, what is love? A question that has been asked by so many. A question that can have so many answers!

Love can vary, let us say the love that you have for your husband/wife, boyfriend/girlfriend or partner is different from the love that you have for your children/parents. Likewise, the love that you may have for nice things; such as food, cars and clothing is different from the love that you have for pets.

I chose the title for this book, *Love Beyond Love,* because the love that my late wife Sharon and I had, really was a love that I had not experienced ever before. For me, love is a feeling of complete contentment and happiness.

This doesn't mean that I have never loved or been loved. I have been married before, which you shall read about later, and I've also had a few relationships over the years, which you won't be reading about!

This book is my story of that love; it will hopefully make you smile from time to time as you begin to flick through the pages. But a word of warning: it will also bring tears to your eyes, as it has me, whilst reminiscing and putting my thoughts and memories into words. In the later chapters, it will be about how I am coping and slowly rebuilding my life and moving forward as Sharon wanted me to.

I began writing this book on 17 November 2018, a special date because it is Sharon's birthday. When it is completed, I shall date the final page.

One thing I will say to you all; I have never written a book before and have no experience in this field. My English lessons at school and exam results were poor. Please bear this in mind and I apologise in advance if there are any grammar or spelling mistakes. You will also notice that I switch between tenses when I write, such as 'Sharon was or Sharon is'. Not good English, I know, but it helps me describe the events which have taken place. My wife died and her physical body is no longer here, but her spirit will always live on, guiding me and watching out for me; she will never be gone from my thoughts and will stay in my heart for always.

Chapter One
Way Back When

As with all love stories, there is always a beginning, so where do I start? I guess I should take you back to the very beginning way back when I was born on Friday, 28 April 1967. I'm lucky to say that both my parents are still with us and that they have been a great support to me, not just in recent years but for all my life.

When I entered this world, there was my mum, dad and my sister, Janice, who was two and a half years old. I was born at home, home being a council flat in Elm Park, Hornchurch Essex. In future years on my sixteenth birthday, I visited the flat. Coincidently, my girlfriend at the time was babysitting for someone who lived there. It felt strange looking around the tiny top floor flat, knowing that sixteen years earlier I had taken my first breaths there.

My dad was always hard working and he worked in the timber preservation trade, which is the treatment of woodworm, dry and wet rot, and rising damp. As a child I couldn't wait for school holidays to come as my dad would sometimes take me to work with him, in his Bedford van. If memory serves me right, it had an engine cover in the front between the driver's seat and passenger seat. It was always hot to touch, great in winter months but very hot and uncomfortable in the hot summer months. (Ok, I know it's the United Kingdom, but I really do remember our summers seemed much hotter back then.) I can still smell the chemicals that my dad would spray about when I think of those times. Empty houses and sometimes mansions, there I was busy sweeping floors and helping in whatever way I could. Lunch times consisted of a cup of tea from a blue tartan thermos flask and a Mr Kipling apple pie, which back then were so much bigger and tastier.

My mum had a difficult time giving birth to me. Apparently, I was twenty-eight days overdue. That's right; I should have been born on April fool's day the 1st. According to my mum and dad, my birth weight was almost 12lb. I say almost because apparently, I broke the midwife's scales.

Over the years, every girlfriend of mine that my dad has met got told the same story. I never get tired of hearing it. Recently, whilst my parents were visiting Sharon's grave, my dad once again decided to tell her the story. I would imagine Sharon was wetting herself with laughter. So here for you all to read in my dad's words is the story of my birth.

"The midwife asked me to boil up the surgical utensils in a saucepan." *Twenty minutes later I asked if I could turn off the gas stove and she promptly replied, "Oh no Stanley, I will tell you when its time."*

"The kitchen now resembled a modern-day steam room with condensation on every surface. Russell was born and I was told to put bricks under one end of the cot, so that his blood would go back to his head.

The midwife then handed me a plastic carrier bag containing a very large placenta. I was told that I had to go and burn it.

So, as darkness fell, I made my way over to some nearby wasteland, where I dug a hole in the ground and placed the bag along with some newspaper and set fire to it with a box of matches. As the fire took hold, the wind began to pick up and the smoke followed me wherever I sat."

According to my mum, Dad returned home later that evening smelling of smoke and his face blackened with soot.

Chapter Two
From Flat to Bungalow

When I was around twelve months old, the Webb family moved to a three-bedroom council bungalow in Ford Lane, Rainham Essex. This was to become my home for the next nineteen years until I moved out.

The bungalow was newly built and was of a Scandinavian style, with sloping roofs and internal ceilings. It overlooked a large playing field; this was where my love of the countryside and open spaces began. I would often sit outside or look through the window staring and thinking. Seasons became real as I watched the spring leaves on the trees start to grow and again turn brown and fall in the autumn months.

My thoughts as a child from the age of about five to fourteen were very mixed up and all over the place, as you will discover in the next chapter.

Our bungalow back in the 1970s had no central heating system, there was however, an electric storage type heater, which blew out warm air but only in one room, the lounge. The winters seemed cold, and on icy mornings, I would wake up to frozen net curtains and ice patterns on my bedroom window. It was quite amusing for me to write my name in the ice and draw faces.

Our home was generally a happy place to live and I have many fond memories of the time I spent in the bungalow in Ford Lane; however, it is also tarnished with sad memories.

Chapter Three
New Arrival

In the previous chapters, I haven't spoken about my sister Janice. We were typical brother and sister, we would play lots and we also had fights, but we loved each other. There were many occasions that Janice and I had to fend for ourselves, and were pushed from pillar to post, with different people looking after us. This was no fault of my parents as at times they had no choice, as you will soon find out.

Our brother Steven was born on 10 December 1970. Mum was in the maternity unit in Rush Green hospital, Romford. (There is now a housing estate on the site where this hospital once stood.) In those days, mothers would generally stay in hospital for a few days, unlike today where women, after childbirth, are mostly in and out in the same day.

It was a couple of weeks before Christmas, so before Mum came home with our new brother; Dad, Janice and me put up the festive decorations. Paper chains as it was then, and artificial 6ft green tree with coloured lights and tinsel. It was soon to become a tradition that the Christmas decorations would be put up on or around Steven's birthday, a tradition that Janice and I still do in our respective homes.

I shared a bedroom with my brother, Steven, and we had many happy times playing hide and seek. Our favourite games were playing house behind the sofa.

Steven was about two years old, when we would play outside. There was a low-level ranch style wooden fence, which surrounded the bungalow. It was on this fence that Steven and I would fold ourselves over, with the timber plank pushing into our tummies. It was around this time that Steven became ill. A tummy ache, I was told.

Janice and I were now walking to and from school on our own. I was just six years old and in the infants' school and Janice was in the junior school. We had no choice, Dad had to work, and Mum was every day, travelling up to St Bartholomew's Hospital in London, to be with Steven. Steven did come home occasionally, but he was very ill. He had lost his pure white blonde hair.

On 14 June 1974, at around 07.00hrs, I was woken up by the sound of the telephone, followed shortly by screams from my mum and the sound of my dad crying.

My brother Steven died age just three and a half years.

For the next seven years, I blamed myself for his death, thinking that I had killed him. I thought and believed that Steven had died from a tummy ache, caused whilst we were playing outside, on that ranch style fence.

I'm not religious and don't practise any faith, however Janice, Steven and myself were all christened under the Church of England.

Every night I would lay awake and pray, seeking forgiveness from these people called Jesus and God, that I had learnt about at school.

I do remember seeing Steven's spirit not long after he had passed. It was early one morning as I went out of the bedroom and looked along the length of the hallway, which seemed a lot longer than normal, and there standing at the end was my brother. Whether this was a dream I had or was Steven's spirit, I'm not entirely sure, but it has stayed a vivid memory for all my life.

At the age of fourteen, I became ill myself. My skin and the whites of my eyes turned yellow in colour. I was also violently vomiting and had a severe headache. I had contracted hepatitis, a liver infection which was highly contagious. I was isolated at home for five weeks, fantastic no school for five whole weeks, but I would have rather been at school.

It was during my illness that my mum told me that my brother Steven had died from cancer; testicular cancer which had spread to his liver and other parts of his tiny body.

For seven long years, I had blamed myself for Steven's death, which I hid from everyone. I was scared and frightened.

Suddenly, I felt a weight lift from my shoulders, all those fears and dark thoughts which I carried for seven years disappeared.

I don't blame my parents, for not telling me about the cancer when Steven was ill; they were trying to protect me from this nasty disease. But I wished they had told me sooner; I could have understood it, and not carried that pain and fear for all those years.

It was only recently that I have spoken about this to my sister.

What Janice and I experienced as children has stayed with us all our lives. There was no child counselling available then; if there was, it was never offered.

Janice and I were looked after by our neighbours, while Mum was at the hospital visiting Steven and Dad was at work. At weekends, we were looked after by our grandads.

On some occasions, we were taken to Saint Bartholomew's Hospital in the heart of London. Steven was on Kenton ward. I remember the elevator which took us up to the floor; it used to scare me. It was the type of elevator which had metal concertina sliding doors; as the elevator went up you could see the floors disappearing and the next one appearing. The smell of grease from the lift shaft, mixed with the smell of disinfectant from the wards lingered in the air.

Janice and I would spend all day sitting outside the ward, it was cold, and you could hear our voices echo. We weren't allowed on the ward to see our brother. At the time, no explanation was given, thinking about it now, I can only assume it was because of the risk of cross contamination.

At the time, we didn't know this and had no idea why we had to stay in the corridor.

On some occasions, we were allowed in the playroom and I can still remember the last ever time that I saw my brother, we were all playing together. A happy time and a happy memory.

Speaking to Janice recently, we remembered those days and the very sick children on the ward. There was one girl that I will never forget, she was very poorly and had to wear a protective helmet. As a child I had no idea why she had this helmet. Now I can only assume that she had surgery for brain cancer.

I often wonder if any of those sick children survived and are with us today. I certainly hope so.

Steven aged 2 years on holiday at Butlins, 1973

Chapter Four
Depression to Joy

As you could imagine, it was a very difficult time for the Webb family. My mum and dad had lost their son and my sister and I had lost our brother.

My parents did their best to conceal their grief and pain from my sister and I, which in itself must have been so difficult for them. Thankfully, they had a group of friends who were really supportive and involved them on social gatherings.

Speaking recently to my mum and dad about my loss, they told me that even after all the years which have passed since Steven died, it still feels very raw and like it happened just yesterday. I can fully understand what they mean by that.

Steven died on 14 June 1974 at 07.00hrs. Three years later on 14 June 1977 at 07.30hrs, my mum gave birth to a baby girl. A coincidence that it was that same date and my parents certainly didn't plan for my sister to be born on the exact same date.

My sister was named Angela, because within its spelling an Angel can be seen.

Prior to Angela's birth, Mum, Dad, Janice, and myself would always visit Steven's grave on a Sunday morning before dinner. The white marble heart shaped headstone shone so bright; sky blue glass chippings cover the length of the grave.

I remember, as a child, going to fill the metal watering cans from the water butt, which had collected rainwater. In the winter months, I had to break the ice to get to the water below.

Our weekly visits to the grave, became less and less after Angela was born. As an adult I often visit my brother's grave, the once bright white marble has weathered and some of the lettering is beginning to peel away. The sky-blue glass chippings still reflect the sunlight. It feels strange standing as an adult at Steven's grave, remembering my childhood Sundays. Nearby my grandparents (dad's parents) also lay at rest and I always pay my respects to them.

Chapter Five
Holidays

My first holiday was a week spent in Butlins Holiday Centre in Clacton on Sea, Essex. I reckon this must have been in 1971. Mum, Dad, Janice, Steven, and I had a wonderful time. We entered fancy dress competitions and bet on the donkey derby. Janice and I spent a lot of the time swimming, mostly in the pools and sometime in the sea. The outdoor pool was massive and unheated, but we were like ducks and the cold didn't bother us.

The holiday centre was very large with rows and rows of chalets where holiday makers would stay. Back then you could leave your baby in the chalet and tie a handkerchief to the front door, then go out to the night-time entertainment. Security would occasionally do patrols, and if they heard a baby crying, they would send a radio message through to their controller. The entertainments team would then make an announcement over the sound system, 'Baby Crying in Chalet number 27', or whatever the number was. It would then be written on a board in white chalk next to the stage, in case you missed the verbal announcements. I do remember Mum rushing back to our chalet on a couple of occasions, to sort Steven out. It is hard to believe that this was normal behaviour back then. It certainly wouldn't happen today. (Now I'm sounding and feeling really old.)

We had another two-week holiday at Butlins a year later, which must have been just before Steven became ill.

My dad knew someone at his work who owned a bungalow in Preston Road, Holland on Sea, Essex, which is just up the coast from Clacton on Sea. We had holidays in the bungalow in 1974, (just two months after Steven died), and also in the following two years. The weather always seemed to be hot and sunny, and we would spend all day at the beach, with a packed lunch and orange squash to drink.

Mum and Dad always tried so hard to make things nice for Janice and myself.

I have many fond memories of our holidays in Clacton and Holland on Sea, and those places will always be special to me.

Today Janice lives a short distance from where Butlins once stood, and my mum and dad live not far from the bungalow in Preston Road, Holland on Sea.

Once Angela was born our holidays in Holland on Sea stopped, and we went further up the east coast to Caister Holiday centre, near Great Yarmouth.

The date was August 1977, when Donna Summer, the female singer, was in the charts with *I Feel Love*. I know this because they played it repeatedly in the clubhouse. Every time Janice and I hear that song it reminds us of that holiday.

Other holiday destinations were Scarborough, Burnham on Sea and Weymouth.

Chapter Six
Teenage Years

As a teenager, I was quite shy when it came to girls. I remember lots of boys in school had girlfriends, and some would come into lessons, boasting about what they had got up to with whoever.

I, on the other hand, was different; yes, there were lots of girls at school that I liked but never wanted to take it any further. I enjoyed their friendship.

Thanks to social media, I am friends with lots of my school mates, both male and female. Reading their comments on my posts that I have written on social media, it appears that I was well liked at school.

I left school at the age of sixteen with poor exam results. Back then it was O levels and CSEs, and I managed to get one O level in woodwork and low grade CSE results in all other subjects. It wasn't that I didn't try; I did put time and effort into my course work but just found written exams difficult.

Since the age of ten, I had been doing karate lessons twice a week. I was flexible and fit and into the whole martial arts scene. Bruce Lee was my hero, and I would go with my dad to the cinema, to watch his films.

At the age of fourteen, I became interested in CB (citizens band) radio. This is basically a radio that you can receive and transmit on, which enables you to communicate with two or more people. I gave myself the handle (CB nickname) of 'Little Dragon'. Bruce Lee was known as this, and due to my interest in martial arts, I thought it was quite apt.

As a CB enthusiast, I soon made many new friends. Back in the 1980s, CB was a big thing and apart from the initial outlay for the equipment, to use CB was free, hence it appealed to so many. Remember mobile phones did not exist then. CB clubs were also a big thing, which was a place where enthusiasts would meet up and socialise.

My local CB club was known as the RBC (Rainham Breakers Club). It was here that I met up with my new friends, and to this day, I am still in contact with them via a different method, called social media.

My CB friends and I would go out for day trips and go to nightclubs, a favourite was called Options nightclub which was next to the Dick Turpin Pub on the A127, just past Basildon. This was our Thursday night entertainment. Tuesday nights were RBC nights and Sunday nights were at the New World Hotel in Brentwood, they had a late licence and had a disco. We would also meet up around each other's homes.

The RBC entered street carnivals and helped raise money for many charities. We also took part in the Southend on Sea raft race, in aid of the Royal National Lifeboat Institution (RNLI). We had so many good times and I can honestly say that my teenage years were great, thanks to my wonderful friends.

Chapter Seven
More Than a Holiday Romance

In July 1985, when I was eighteen years old, my CB friends and I went on a two-week holiday to Devon, and it was here that I met Tina, a 24-year-old woman from Winchester in Hampshire. She was holidaying with her parents and sister.

My holiday with my friends was great, but looking back now, I did tend to leave them, to spend time with Tina.

This was to continue, and my network of friends, that I had had from the age of fourteen, were soon left out as I began to spend more and more time with Tina, travelling back and forward from Rainham to Winchester on most weekends.

I have no regrets meeting Tina, but I do regret dropping everything for her and losing contact with my good friends. This being my fault entirely.

I am glad that I am back in contact with my friends on Facebook and their comments to my posts are really comforting. Thank you so much for being there for me.

Tina and I continued seeing each other, and on Valentine's Day 1987 we got engaged. A few months later we got a first-time buyer's mortgage and moved into a two bedroomed house in Basildon, Essex.

I had my twenty first birthday party in that home. It feels strange that both our children have also had their twenty first birthdays there.

In the late 1980s, the mortgage interest rates went sky high, fortunately I was on a reasonable wage and managed, but at times it was difficult.

Chapter Eight
My Work

As I have mentioned wages, I guess that it's only right that I talk about my employment history.

I left school in 1983 aged sixteen, and back then it was difficult to get an apprenticeship, unless you completed twelve months on the Youth Training Scheme (YTS).

So, after a few months of working as a labourer on building sites, I started on the YTS in the September. Which consisted of six months in college and six months in a joinery factory. I was learning the basic skills of becoming a carpenter and joiner. I always had an interest in carpentry, which stems from my childhood when I used to help my dad.

Whilst on the YTS, the Government paid me a whopping twenty-five pounds a week. After I completed the scheme, the joinery company offered me an apprenticeship, as a carpenter and joiner, and I learnt my trade in an old-fashioned joinery factory, which made high class, bespoke joinery items for a variety of clients.

One project I was involved in, which sticks in my mind, is the hardwood lattice benches which sit outside the Bank of England in London. I was part of the team who made them in the factory and was lucky enough to fit them together on site. To this day they are still there, they look weathered and some have been replaced but we are talking approximately thirty-five years ago.

I completed my apprenticeship and stayed with the company for a further six months and then moved to another joinery firm, where I worked on the Chelsea Harbour project. I was soon made joinery foreman and oversaw a team of carpenters.

On completion of the works in Chelsea, I was moved to another site near to Fenchurch Street, which was great, because I didn't have to travel across London on the underground trains.

It was whilst I was on this project that I was approached by the management company, and was asked to work for them as a contracts manager. The offer was too good to refuse; a company car, expenses paid, private health care and a good salary. I enjoyed working on multimillion-pound contracts in London and met some amazing tradesmen.

In 1991/92, the financial recession hit the building trade hard, and at the beginning of 1992 I was made redundant, so I needed to find a job with more security.

I applied for the position as a fire fighter, and on 27 April 1992, I started training with the London Fire Brigade and I still currently work for them. I enjoy my job and as you can imagine I have seen and dealt with many nasty things over the years, but have also saved lives which is very rewarding. I could write lots about my time as a fire fighter, however, I think I will save that for another potential book at a later date.

Chapter Nine
My First Wedding

Tina and I got married on 21 July 1990, which was a blazing hot summer's day. The wedding itself was a traditional type, we married in St Helen and St Giles Church in Rainham, and our reception was in a social hall in the same village.

The Church happens to be the same Church where my mum and dad were married in 1964, and it's also where I was christened as a baby.

Our wedding day was lovely and we honeymooned in Menorca. I had never flown before or been to a hot country, so it was a lovely experience.

As I am writing this chapter, I look back and see that I haven't written much; however, this doesn't mean that my wedding day and honeymoon weren't special to me; they really were and I have many fond memories.

Chapter Ten
Our Children

About a year after our wedding, we decided to try for a family, bear in mind that we had been together since 1985, and hadn't used any form of contraception.

It was now 1993 and still, there was no success and it was at this point that we visited our doctors and were put on an IVF programme.

Now if any of you readers have experienced this, I think you will agree that it takes the fun out of love making. Regular visits to the maternity unit, temperature taking and ultrasound examinations, the list goes on and on. A lot of pressures and expectations which affect both the man and woman.

Thankfully, with the help of medication and temperature taking, Tina fell pregnant in 1994, and on 16 March 1995, our son Jason, was born.

Unfortunately, not long after our son's birth, he became poorly and was taken to the special care baby unit. It was so difficult for us to come home without Jason. Everything was in place; I had put banners and balloons up, saying 'It's a Boy'. But we came home empty-handed. Thankfully, Jason made a full recovery and we were eventually able to bring him home about five days later.

As I was doing shift work, I was able to spend a lot of time with my family, probably more than most working fathers who do a Monday to Friday 9 to 5 job. In saying that, my shift work does mean I have to work nights, weekends, Christmas, and Easter.

Three years after Jason was born, we decided to try for another child. Again, we had to go through the same IVF process as before. More tests and more clinical procedures which was a stressful time for us both.

Thankfully, again with the help of medication and more temperature taking, Tina became pregnant in 1998 and on 5 March 1999, we had a beautiful daughter.

It was Jason who named our daughter. At the time, he was going to pre-school and his teacher was named Maria. Jason could not pronounce her name properly and when he said it, it came out sounding like teacher Mia. Tina and I liked the name so that became our daughter's name.

I remember Tina saying to me not long after Mia was born, that she would love a third child at some point.

We brought our daughter home and we began our lives as a family of four.

Chapter Eleven
Close to Death

Two weeks after Mia was born, Tina was still in a lot of pain. Her GP treated her for an infection and arranged for an ultrasound of the womb.

The results of the ultrasound showed that part of the placenta had been left behind. Tina was then referred to the maternity unit for a D and C (Dilation and Curettage). A common procedure which, without going into too much detail, is a surgical procedure which is used to remove parts of the lining or contents of the uterus.

Tina went off to have the procedure and I waited in the waiting room. I was told that Tina would return in about an hour and a half.

The waiting room was small, in fact it was more like a waiting area rather than a room. Four hard blue plastic chairs, rigid and fixed together. Opposite was a mirror image. A small table to one side with out-of-date magazines, a discarded toddlers' dummy, pink in colour lay on the floor.

It's amazing what you take in, but when you are stuck in the same chair for three and a half hours; you begin to remember every single detail.

At the two hour point, I asked a nurse how Tina was, nobody came back to tell me. Three hours had now passed, and I was rather concerned, luckily, I managed to find another nurse and ask. This time she came back and said that Tina's blood pressure was unstable.

Thirty minutes later I remember seeing Tina being pushed on a trolley, she was laying down and was white in colour, and looked very unwell. By now, I was holding Tina's hand, Doctors and nurses surrounded the bed. Tina looked at me and said, "Russell, I feel as though I'm bleeding."

With that, a nurse lifted the sheet to reveal a heavily blood-soaked gown. The surgeon who performed the D and C had lacerated her womb. Tina was now bleeding internally and externally; her major organs were beginning to shut down. It was now a matter of life or death.

Tina had to go to the operating theatre, I remember pushing the trolley with the surgeons and nurses. We were running along a long corridor. The fluorescent ceiling lights flashing as we went past each one. It was like a scene from a movie.

Tina had to be anesthetised on the operating table because there was no time for proper procedures.

The theatre doors slammed, and I was left standing in the corridor, there was an eerie silence. Twenty minutes later a nurse came out and took me to a purpose-built relatives' room. There were no hard chairs, instead there were two soft high back ones, this time the small table had a vase with fake flowers, a box of tissues and a bible. There was a small kitchen area with microwave, kettle and tea/coffee making facilities. And there was a single bed. I was told to wait in this room.

After about two and a half hours, a doctor and nurse entered my room. I was told that to save my wife's life and stop the bleed, they had to do an emergency hysterectomy, as the laceration was too big to repair.

Tina had lost so much blood her major organs had begun to shut down. I wasn't allowed to see her as she had been moved to intensive care, and was on a machine which was breathing for her, she was placed in an induced coma.

I was told to stay in the room and expect the worst. Tina was very ill.

So, there I sat feeling numb and alone, my wife could possibly die, my thoughts went to my children. What would I tell them? How could I tell them? I left the room to find a pay phone, I called my mum who was looking after Jason and Mia. I also called Tina's parents and gave them the news.

My time in the relatives' room felt like a prison sentence. I sat in the chair feeling alone and scared. I didn't sleep at all, every noise I heard, I thought it was the Doctors coming to give me bad news.

Morning eventually came and I was finally able to see Tina. She was still in intensive care and had lots of tubes and wires connected to her. The machine was still breathing for her.

The doctors then slowly began to wake Tina up and the breathing machine was turned off. I watched the tube being removed from her throat. Thankfully, Tina gasped and began to breathe on her own.

Tina remained in hospital for about a week, she had endured a major life saving operation and needed time to heal. Several weeks passed before she was able to lift anything, including our baby daughter.

The coming weeks and months were very difficult for us both. The trauma of Tina almost dying and losing her ability to have any more children, had certainly left a mental scar with both of us.

Our relationship also suffered, and it was twelve months later that I made the decision to leave my wife. This was the hardest decision that I have ever made in my entire life.

Tina and I remain friends and I can honestly say that I have the upmost respect for her. She has and continues to be a good mother to our children.

Although I left Tina, I never walked away from my children and my responsibilities as their father, and even now that they are both adults, they both know that I shall always be there for them.

Chapter Twelve
The 'Single' Years

In the fourteen years from leaving Tina to meeting Sharon, I had other relationships, two of which each lasted around three years. The other times, I was generally single, going out on dates here and there.

Regarding homes, I moved in with my first girlfriend and lived with her family and as I have already said, we lasted around three years. Following on from that, I was pretty much homeless, spending many cold nights sleeping in my car, parked up on a country lane. Two nights out of eight, I would be at the fire station on night shift.

I met my next girlfriend in a supermarket, and it wasn't long before I moved in with her. After about a year, we decided to rent a home together in a little village just outside of Chelmsford. We spent just over two years in that cottage in Roxwell. Our relationship broke down and we split up.

My next home was in a small one bedroomed house in another village called Bicknacre, the opposite side of Chelmsford. This was the first time that I had lived on my own in my own home. I had a tropical fish tank and would spend many nights watching the colourful fish swimming around, which I found far more relaxing than watching the rubbish on television.

It was a year later when I purchased a three bedroomed static caravan on a park in Battlesbridge.

This was to become my home for the next four years. Jason and Mia loved spending time here, it was like a holiday for them. On the site, there was a club house with entertainment at weekends, an outdoor swimming pool and amusement arcade. During the winter months it was rather bleak, sometimes the water pipes would freeze, and it was extremely difficult to keep my caravan warm.

During the cold season I didn't have my children stay with me, instead I would pick them up and we would go out for days.

Unfortunately, the park management changed and the static caravans gradually, one by one, were taken away and replaced with new modern double unit park homes.

So, I had to go back to renting privately, and moved to a lovely cottage situated between Billericay and Basildon, which had outstanding countryside views. This became my home for the next four years.

I was really happy in this cottage, each morning I would wake up and watch the changing seasons of the countryside from my bedroom window. The beautiful sunsets are outstanding

But something was missing; I felt lonely, so I started to search an online dating website, in search for companionship, which I hoped would turn to love. There were a few women that I dated, which lasted a few months. Apart from that, you could say that I was single most of the time.

I was beginning to think that perhaps I was going to be single forever. At work one day, I told my friends that I never wanted to live with another woman and will never marry again. However, deep down, I was feeling lost and empty.

When I wasn't working or seeing my children and family, I would spend time alone. Sometimes, I would take a drive out to Westcliff near Southend on Sea, and just walk along the sea front for a change of scenery. Of course, when I'm in Southend, I must always stop at Rossi's Ice Cream Parlour, and get a large vanilla cornet with a chocolate flake.

Nearby, there is a wooden bench at the top of some steps, I named this Russell's bench, as I would often sit there and look out over the sea, taking in every detail that I could see around me. On occasions, I would take a book and read, but to be honest I prefer to just look and get lost in my own thoughts.

Night times at home were lonely, I didn't really watch TV, mostly, I would listen to music or lay outside and star gaze. I am fascinated by the night skies and on occasions I would spend hours just looking up and taking it all in. I just wished I had someone next to me, to appreciate it with.

My dad used to say to me, "One day Russell, you will meet the perfect woman, who will be right for you."

Chapter Thirteen
The First Messages

It was Thursday, 4 September 2014, and I was on night shift at the fire station.

All the checks of the appliance and equipment are complete, we have had a lecture and it was around 23.00 hrs.

It was then when I switched my phone on and began to scroll through the pages of Plenty of Fish, the dating website, continuing my search for love. After five minutes or so, I stopped at one particular black and white photo, and straight away, I was drawn to the beautiful smile of this woman. After reading her profile, I decided to send a message to this lovely lady. To be honest, I wasn't expecting to get a reply.

The photo on the next page is Sharon's "Plenty of Fish" profile photo. I can honestly say that after just one look at her photo and her beautiful smile, I was well and truly hooked

Sharon replied soon after and for the next hour or so we spoke via messages. I wish I still had those first messages because it would be lovely to look back on them. Unfortunately, when I deleted my POF account all messages were also deleted.

We exchanged phone numbers and I asked Sharon if it would be ok for me to call her in the morning, when I finished my night shift. She replied "Yes, that will be lovely."

Morning came and I was so excited about phoning Sharon. I made sure that my phone was fully charged before I left work. It would have been about 09.45hrs, when I first heard the voice of the woman I was going to fall in love with and would end up marrying.

We probably spoke for over an hour about anything and everything, I felt so at ease. We decided to meet up after the weekend.

Over the next two days we sent many text messages to each other.

It was Sharon who chose where we were to meet on our first date, this being the *Dandelion Coffee Shop,* in the quaint village of Stock.

Chapter Fourteen
The First Date

Monday 8 September 2014. A date which will stay in my heart and in my thoughts for always.

We had arranged to meet at 10.00hrs; however, Sharon messaged me saying she would be about half hour late, as her ex had turned up at her house and wanted to talk.

I have always been one for getting to meetings early and don't like being late. Today was no different, I arrived at the coffee shop at 09.45hrs, forty-five minutes early! I was just so excited about meeting Sharon.

I parked my car in the narrow lane and waited, checking my rear-view mirror every time a car approached. The weather was sunny, and the skies were blue. At 10.30hrs, a car pulled up behind me, which was Sharon's. I got out of my car first and waited for Sharon to get out of hers.

My first thoughts were, WOW! She is stunning and how lucky am I to be here on a date with this beautiful woman.

She was wearing a dark navy-blue pencil skirt, which was just above her knees, and a pastel pink blouse with small flowers printed on the fabric. Draped over her arm was a cardigan, and she was wearing sandals on her feet. Her blonde shoulder length hair shimmered in the sunlight as it caught the gentle breeze.

We both said hello and smiled, then I kissed her softly on her cheek before crossing the road and going into the coffee shop.

We sat at a round table; the chairs were positioned opposite each other. I asked what Sharon wanted, then placed the order for two medium lattes.

Our conversation did not once dry up, we spoke of our children, our work, holidays, and many other things. I learnt that Sharon was a Health Care Support Worker, on a care for the elderly ward at Broomfield Hospital, Chelmsford.

I guess that we remained in the coffee shop for about two hours. You could feel the energy between us, our knees were touching under the table. I felt very relaxed and comfortable, a feeling that I had not experienced on other dates before. Outside, the sun was still shining, so I suggested to Sharon we could go to Southend on Sea for a walk and a bite to eat. Sharon left her car parked outside the coffee shop and we headed off in my car.

The journey time was around forty minutes, which on the way passed the top end of the road where I lived, and I spoke of the amazing countryside views. By now, in between changing gears, we were holding hands and it was when we were almost at Southend, whilst stopping at traffic lights that we had our first proper kiss. Nowadays, when I drive down that road and wait at the same lights I always think of that time, and I relive that special moment.

I parked the car near to the Chalkwell end of Southend and we began to walk along the sea front in the direction of Westcliff, we were holding hands and occasionally we would stop and just hold each other. The tide was in, which pleased me, because it looks so much nicer when the mud is covered up.

Our lunch stop was to be at one of the cafes which are known as 'The Arches'. For many years, I have been going here and would take my children. I always made a game out of which one we would eat in; with Jason and Mia having to choose. The red one? The blue one? The yellow one? The brown one? The striped one? But not the floral one! The colours representing the colour of the cafe/restaurant awnings. Even to this day, when I go there with my children, who are now adults, we must choose and who ever chose last time is excluded. I think it is my turn to choose next!

Sharon and I stopped at the yellow one and we sat outside overlooking the sea. We had jacket potato with prawns and a side salad. I remember feeling like I had known this woman a lot longer than just a few hours.

After, we carried on walking and reached the Rossi ice-cream parlour. Like I said earlier, whenever in Southend, it's rude not to indulge in a Rossi's. I had the usual, a large vanilla cornet with chocolate flake, and Sharon had medium vanilla ice cream with flake, but in a tub.

We carried on walking until we reached "Russell's" bench. I wanted to share my special place with Sharon, so we sat together eating our ice cream and looking out over the estuary. The golden sun was turning the gentle waves into a sea of sparkling gold. I told Sharon that this was the bench that I would often sit on alone, it was at that point that I looked her in the eyes, held her hand and said that from that day it would always be known as 'Sharon and Russell's Bench'.

Whilst there on our bench we spoke lots, laughed, kissed, and cuddled, yet there were also times when we held hands and just simply enjoyed the view.

Even though there would have been cars driving along the road and people walking, I don't remember seeing them because I was just focused on Sharon and the wonderful sea view.

It was late afternoon when we decided to head back to Stock so that Sharon could collect her car, however, on the way back as we approached the road where I lived, I asked if I could make Sharon a cup of tea and show her the countryside views.

I showed Sharon around my cottage and made us both a tea. Now, it was the bedroom in my cottage that had the best views, so this is how we ended up sitting on the edge of my bed drinking tea and taking in the spectacular countryside views.

On the journey back to Stock from my house, we spoke more and talked about seeing each other again and we arranged to meet on the Thursday. I stopped my car just behind Sharon's car and we held each other in our arms and kissed again. As we said our goodbyes, I asked Sharon to txt me when she arrived home safely; which she did.

On the way back home, I was on a high, I couldn't stop thinking about the wonderful day we had. Later that night we spoke again on the phone and sent messages and it must have been around 01.30hrs when I eventually went to sleep. The next two days, Tuesday and Wednesday, I was on duty at the fire station, doing day shifts but that didn't stop us from messaging each other and speaking on the phone.

I couldn't wait to see Sharon again and I was so excited about our second date.

Thursday came, and Sharon drove to my house and we decided to drive to Southend again for lunch. We were so lucky with the weather; it was sunny and warm. In fact, whenever Sharon and I went away for short breaks and holidays the sun always shone down on us.

Chapter Fifteen
Sharon's Family

Whilst on our first and second dates, we learnt a lot about each other. I spoke about my children, Jason and Mia, and about the rest of my family.

Sharon told me about her three children which are all of adult age and spoke of her four grandchildren. Sharon loved to spend time with her grandchildren, taking them out for days and having them around for sleepovers.

In fact, Sharon was very much family orientated and would always be the one arranging family gatherings, such as summer barbecues and Sunday roasts.

Although Sharon had told her family about me, she was concerned that it may have caused them to be upset, meeting me face to face, too soon after she had split up from their father.

I didn't get to meet Sharon's children until the April of 2015, when we had a family afternoon trip to the local ten pin bowling alley.

I didn't meet Sharon's eldest son, until the November of 2015, when he came to our house to pick his children up.

As far as I know and from what Sharon told me, there was some sort of upset between the two of them and to this day I really don't know what the issues were. It would be wrong of me to comment any more about this, or to make any assumptions, however, I am so pleased to say that they both sorted things out in September 2016.

I was lucky to be able to meet Sharon's parents. Her mum lived in Chelmsford and her dad lived in Bicknacre. Sharon was the youngest of three children.

As I got to know the family, I felt accepted by them and as my love for Sharon grew so did my love for her family. Sharon and I really enjoyed the times when both our families got together.

I have already mentioned that it was six months before I met Sharon's family, therefore it was awkward for me to go to Chelmsford to see Sharon at her house. Unfortunately, it was left to Sharon to drive to me. This was totally against the grain for me, because I believe that it should be the man picking his girlfriend up and taking her home safely. This may sound old fashioned but it's what my dad taught me and is something that I have always done.

The journey from Sharon's home to my home took around thirty minutes; on parts of the journey there are no streetlights and tall trees stand along each side, which block out any natural moon light. So, one of the first things I did was to order and fit new brighter head light bulbs for Sharon's car. Whenever Sharon got home or to work, I would always get her to call me, to let me know she had arrived safely.

There were times when I met Sharon at the end of her road and we went out to a nearby countryside pub, and as it was winter, the open fire was lit. We sat for ages, talking and holding hands in the flickering orange glow.

There were two occasions when I did go to Sharon's home and stay overnight. This was when Sharon's son was staying with his girlfriend.

Chapter Sixteen
A True Angel

It was in the middle of October 2014 that my mum was admitted into hospital. She had been suffering for some time with confusion caused by a urinary tract infection. As well as this, my mum has multiple sclerosis and suffers with trigeminal neuralgia, which is a sudden and severe facial pain, sometimes described as an electric shock type pain in the jaw and mouth. For this, my mum was on a cocktail of pain-relieving drugs.

It was during this time, whilst my mum was in hospital, that Sharon first met my dad. We took him out for dinner one evening to a carvery restaurant in Clacton on Sea. That evening we spoke lots and straight away there was a connection between Dad and Sharon, a connection that I hadn't seen before with other girlfriends that had met my dad. Obviously at this time my dad was so worried about my mum, but Sharon had a way about her, she could cheer anyone up and was able to talk and engage in conversation.

A few days later Sharon and I visited Mum in Clacton Hospital, this being the first time that she had met her. Sharon was so calming, caring, and respectful to my mum. She held her hand and told her all will be fine.

I guess now is a good time to tell you about Sharon's work as an NHS Health Care Support Worker. For fifteen years, Sharon worked at Broomfield Hospital on Braxted Ward, caring for the elderly, this being a job that many would probably steer clear of. Sharon was dedicated to her work and she was well loved amongst her colleagues. These were not just work colleagues, they were her friends outside of work. A true testament of how much Sharon is thought of amongst her work friends, is the solid oak memorial bench that now stands in the ward garden.

In July 2019, ten months after Sharon had passed, I was invited to Braxted ward by her friends to view the bench. This is my account of that day

It feels strange driving back to Broomfield Hospital, I've not been here since Sharon was very poorly. I park the car in the car park, I'm here early, taking my time walking through the atrium and stopping for a coffee. It was here that I used to meet Sharon when she was on her lunch breaks. She mostly would have a healthy salad that she had brought in from home. Moving on, I pass the pharmacy where I have visited so many times, collecting the many drugs that Sharon needed. I continue making my way through the hospital towards Braxted ward and I'm now feeling rather emotional. As I get to the ward the ward clerk who I recognise opens the electronic doors. He greets me by saying, "Hello Russell, how are you? Are you here to see Sharon's Bench?" He tells me to go through to the staff rest room. I see some of Sharon's friends who are obviously working today, I say hello and talk for a little while. As I walk into the staff restroom to access the garden, positioned on the wall above a row of coat hooks is Sharon's NHS identity photo, which has been enlarged and is surrounded by other smaller photos of Sharon with her friends from the ward on various nights out. I spend a moment here looking at the photos and a lump comes to my throat. Moving into the garden I can see a sky-blue painted pergola with honeysuckle growing up each side. There, standing on grey slate chippings is a beautiful solid oak bench. I will sit here for a while and gather my thoughts. The words inscribed within an oak heart on the back rest of the bench are from the song 'A million dreams' from the movie 'The Greatest Showman'.

Our Beautiful Friend Sharon
Dream a million dreams
"However Big. However Small
Let me be part of it all."
You will always be part of our Braxted Family

This beautiful bench is a wonderful lasting tribute to a truly amazing woman. A True Angel.

I thanked Sharon's friends and left the ward and headed back to my car, I felt very emotional, yet I felt so proud to know such a special woman.

Over the first few months of knowing Sharon, I soon realised how much she was loved. She had such a large network of friends, even childhood friends and neighbours that she had grown up with were still in contact. I always encouraged Sharon to see her friends and she generally arranged to meet them when I was on night shifts and by doing it that way, we were able to spend as much time as possible together.

Chapter Seventeen
Brighton Birthday

The first time that we went away was for Sharon's birthday, 17th November 2014. I booked up a two-night hotel in a village outside of Brighton. The room had a four-poster bed and a double ended Jacuzzi bath, in full view of the bed. There was a separate shower room which was huge.

When I booked the hotel, I asked for a bouquet of fresh flowers to be placed in the room for Sharon. We arrived on the 16th, and that night whilst we were at dinner, I said to Sharon that I had to pop back to the room quickly to use the toilet. Of course, this was just a cover, I went to hang Happy Birthday banners around the four-poster bed.

You should have seen Sharon's face when we both went back to the room later that night. I filled the Jacuzzi bath and lit the tealight candles that I had placed around the edge earlier and played soft music through my phone speaker. A glass of wine for Sharon and orange juice for me, we both relaxed in the bath. Now one thing I have learnt…Don't put bubble bath in a Jacuzzi! As soon as I turned the jets on, we were separated by a growing mountain of foaming bubbles, the candles were extinguished and for a moment I lost sight of Sharon. We just couldn't stop laughing, even the next day there were still bubbles all over the place.

The next day, Sharon's birthday, I had set the alarm for 07.30hrs. I made us both a cup of tea which we drank in bed, as I gave Sharon her birthday presents. I had managed to get tickets for the rock band Queen with Adam Lambert, who were playing at the O2 in London, in the coming January. Earlier in this book, I told you of my love for the night time skies, so I decided to have a star named the 'Sharon & Russ Star', I wrapped up a silver framed certificate with the coordinates and star chart showing its location. Coincidently, Sharon had already thought of the idea and had named a star for me, she couldn't tell me about as it was to be a Christmas present for me. Great minds think alike!

After breakfast, we drove to Brighton seafront and parked the car about half a mile past the famous Brighton Pier with the sea on our left-hand side and walked in the direction of the pier. We always held hands, Sharon's right hand in my left, strangely if we ever did it the opposite way round it just didn't feel right. The same applied in bed with Sharon laying on my left-hand side. In theatres, restaurants and cinemas, Sharon would be sitting on my left. When anyone would see us together, looking from the front, Sharon would be on the right-hand side. I used to say, "It was because Sharon was always right."

Even when making a cup of tea or coffee Sharon's cup would be on the right, this was quite useful because she used to have one sweetener, whereas, I have nothing in my tea and coffee.

The weather that day was sunny at times and mild for the time of year. Walking across the pebbles we found a place to sit near to the sea. In fact, we laid down for a while, feeling the sun on our faces and listening to the sound of the waves breaking, moving the rounded pebbles back and forward. It was so relaxing.

After a while, I had the sudden urge to attempt to skim pebbles between the waves. I failed miserably, however Sharon did the most perfect skim, the shiny pebble bouncing, not once or twice, but three times before disappearing. We continued to walk along the promenade, stopping for a coffee along the way. Reaching the pier, we stopped and took a selfie with the Brighton Pier sign in the background.

I always took many photos, videos and selfies, wherever we went and I'm so happy that I was able to capture our special times. Sharon loved to print the photos and place them in albums and nowadays I get great comfort from flicking through the many memories that we made. Although at times it can also be upsetting.

Being as it was November; Brighton Council had erected an outdoor ice-skating rink, in preparation for Christmas and the festive season. Today it was open and naturally we decided to give the skating a go. We had so much fun and I really must admit Sharon was so much better at it than me. Another skater on the ice stopped and took a photo of us. This was the very first photo of us, which isn't a selfie, and you can see this photo on the next page.

When I started to plan this book, I wasn't going to add any photos, however, as I relive the memories within my mind and put pen to paper, I think it would be a nice way to bring my words to life.

After spending the day in Brighton, we headed back to our hotel. We both decided that we didn't want to eat in the restaurant that night, as we wanted to enjoy our room, so I ventured out in search for a takeaway, whilst Sharon relaxed in the Jacuzzi.

About forty-five minutes later I returned armed with a Chinese meal and a bottle of wine. We sat opposite each other around a small circular table and tucked in.

I had already planned dessert by the way of a birthday cake which I had secretly packed in my travel bag before leaving home. The perfect time for me to retrieve this from the bag came when Sharon took the Chinese take away containers to the bathroom to wash them up. I stuck six candles in the chocolate covering, avoiding the edible fondant icing sugar "Happy Birthday" lettering, and lit them. I dimmed the lights and as Sharon came back into the room, I sang the happy birthday song and gave her a kiss and hugged her. One thing that I had forgotten to pack was a knife to cut the cake, so we improvised using the flimsy white plastic one that came with the takeaway.

Next day we went to a quaint tearoom in the village. It had oak beams and a low ceiling, antique toys and old-fashioned photos were placed on shelves and in little alcoves. We ordered a cream tea; warm fruit scones with strawberry jam and real Cornish clotted cream.

It was in this tearoom, where the 'Flux Capacitor' began. Ok, I shall explain. In the movie 'Back to the Future', inside the DeLorean car which they use for time travel there is a flux capacitor. The best way to describe this is imagine drawing a capital letter 'Y'.

Anyway, we had finished our cream teas and I was playing around with the narrow sachets of sugar, placing them on the white linen tablecloth in the shape of a heart and an arrow pointing towards Sharon. Next Sharon decided to return the gesture by doing the same, but needed to use my sugar sachets. Now, the heart that she did was fine but somehow, she had forgotten what an arrow looked like and placed the sachets in the shape of a 'Flux Capacitor'. We laughed so much that others in the tearoom turned around to see what was going on. This wasn't the last of our Flux Capacitor as there were other occasions when it would pop up again and make an appearance.

Sharon's birthday trip to Brighton was lovely in every way and we often spoke about our first time away and laughed as we relived our memories.

Chapter Eighteen
Our First Christmas

Now, I'm going to be honest by saying that I really am not into the whole Christmas thing. To me the most important thing about the 25th December is that it's my Dad's birthday. However, this year I was feeling different and was actually looking forward to our first Christmas together.

Since being a firefighter, I have had to work on many Christmases. However, in 2014 my tour of duty finished on Xmas eve morning. Meaning I had the next four days off.

Anyone who knows me, will know that I like to have a plan, needing to know what I'm doing in advance. It's ok to deviate from the plan as long as another plan is put in its place, if you get my meaning. Sharon was the same and felt the need to have a plan. Now, some would say that's not good as there is the potential for two plans to clash.

This was never the case as our plans became one, just like Sharon and I became one the very first time we set eyes on each other.

So, on the build up to Xmas we made our plan, and this is how our first Christmas went:

On Christmas Eve morning, Sharon was working at the hospital, early shift. I got home from work and finished wrapping Sharon's presents.

A few weeks before, I had handmade a hardwood memory box and varnished it. On the lid, I carved the words *'Memories of Love'*. Sharon soon began to fill the box with special things and memories of things we had done and of places that we had been. The box is now full, and to this date I have not yet looked inside. I will do this when I am ready, and will probably go away for a couple of days, taking the box with me and turning my phone off, to avoid any distractions.

When Sharon finished work, she drove over and got to me in the late afternoon. Our meal that night was nibbles, consisting of cheese and biscuits, cold meats, pickles, crisps, nuts, and a selection of dips for the cucumber and carrots that I had cut into finger sized strips earlier. That night I learnt that

Sharon's favourite cheese was French Brie. We didn't watch television, instead we talked, laughed, listened to music, and even danced.

As Christmas Eve drew to a close, we exchanged presents with Christmas songs playing softly in the background and scented candles flickering, as if in time with the music.

Christmas day came and we were awake early because Sharon was on early shift again at the hospital. Sharon was going to spend the afternoon and evening with her children and grandchildren.

For me, I went to see my mum and dad. My mum hadn't long been home from hospital and I wanted to spend time with them both. The first thing I always do is wish my dad a Happy Birthday. I cooked a three-course traditional Christmas roast dinner, with all the trimmings. After dinner, we sat and watched a DVD, which I had given to Mum as a present; *Simon and Garfunkel Live in Central Park.* As a child, I remember my mum playing the album; Bridge Over Troubled Water, on the old record player that we had back then.

The next day the 26th, in the UK we call it Boxing Day, which is a public holiday, I was home; Jason and Mia, my children, were coming over.

Since leaving my first wife, I have always left Christmas days for my children to be with their mum. Yes, there were times when they could have been with me but I didn't want Tina to be on her own. So generally, I would see Jason and Mia on or around Boxing Day, depending on my shift work at the fire station.

It was around midday when Jason and Mia arrived. Sharon was due to get to me around 14.00hrs.

Remember, that not only was this Christmas different for me, but it was also totally different from what Sharon had been used to. As far as I know, it was a Boxing Day tradition for Sharon and all her family to get together at her mother in law's home.

I cooked another Christmas meal, and the four of us sat around the small pine cottage style dining table. We pulled Christmas crackers and wore the paper hats. I must say the dinner was a success, apart from the sage and onion stuffing which I had forgotten about and left in the bottom of the oven. However, it turned out to be a great 'frisbee' in the garden.

After dinner, we exchanged presents with Jason and Mia and then played games. Sharon loved Christmas games and this year we played a word game which I was absolutely rubbish at, but we did have a laugh though. That night

Jason and Mia were staying over with Sharon and me, we stayed up quite late and we watched a movie on TV.

Next day, we headed off to Lakeside shopping centre, to have a look around the sales and it was here where I bought a smoothie maker (blender). It was Sharon who got me into smoothies. Not long after we had met, I was fitting a kitchen for someone in my off-duty days, and the job happened to be just around the corner to where Sharon lived. Sharon walked to the house where I was working and had kindly made me a packed lunch, consisting of sandwiches, crisps and a strawberry and banana smoothie. Most mornings Sharon would have a smoothie for her breakfast.

Our first New Year's Eve was spent with Sharon's work friend and her husband at a Chinese restaurant, which had a disco and an Elvis Presley impersonator. We danced and sang all night as we welcomed in 2015.

Chapter Nineteen
London Trips

Over the four years that I had with Sharon, we often travelled into London, which takes about 40min by train from Chelmsford.

Our first time in London was on Saturday, 10 January 2015, when we went to see the Christmas lights which were still illuminating Oxford and Regents Street. We got into London Liverpool Street Station in the late afternoon and it was already dark, we took the London Underground tube to Holborn, where we got off and walked to Covent Garden.

Covent Garden was bustling with tourists and people shopping, Christmas lights sparkled, and buskers were performing around a Christmas tree. As we strolled through the under covered market, you could smell the spices from mulled wine. We found a bar just outside the undercover section of the market, which had seating and gas flame patio heaters. Sharon had a hot mulled wine and I had a frothy coffee.

Next, we walked through Leicester Square, taking in the ambience as we headed towards Piccadilly Circus, where we stood in front of the buildings all lit up with neon advertising. And yes, I took a selfie, I wonder how many millions of photos have been taken here over the years. We carried on walking in the direction of Trafalgar Square, then onto Northumberland Avenue heading towards the River Thames. Here we used the Golden Jubilee footbridge, stopping and taking photos. One photo I took of Sharon had the London Eye in the background, in fact it looked like she had a halo above her head. We crossed the Thames and walked along the Southbank towards Tower Bridge, stopping for a bite to eat along the way.

There were other times that we went to the West End, to see shows at the theatre. However, we didn't just go in the evening; we would travel just after the morning rush hour and then make a full day of it, by taking in the sights and sounds of our Capital.

It was on 2 March 2015 when we went on the London Eye. It was a clear sunny day and we could see all the major sights of London. On that day, we also did the Tower Bridge tour; crossing the bridge at high level and seeing how the bridge operated when it first opened.

On my birthday the same year 28 April 2015, Sharon took me to London for the day and surprised me with a visit to the top of The Shard. Again, we were lucky to have good weather and we could see for miles. She then took me for a posh meal in a Borough Market restaurant.

One evening we were talking about the Monarchy and I asked Sharon if she had ever been to Buckingham Palace. She told me that she had never been there, and had only seen it in photos or on TV. I told her about the time when I was a boy, when my grandad took me to London, back then Trafalgar Square was covered with pigeons and pigeon droppings. He took me to watch the changing of the guards at Buckingham Palace. As I was watching I somehow managed to push my head through the iron railings at the front of the Palace, getting my head well and truly wedged. My grandad lifted me upside down and pulled me out, and still to this day, I don't know why he lifted me upside down or even how he managed to get me free. I like to think that it was the skills he learnt from being a soldier in World War Two. I now had a mission to take Sharon to London and show her Buckingham Palace. So, on 11 March 2016, we hopped on the train to London and went to Hyde Park, where we had a coffee next to The Serpentine Lake. We then made our way to Admiralty Arch and into The Mall; I wanted Sharon to experience the red coloured tarmac road, and to see the golden statues as we approached The Palace. We watched the changing of the guards and I showed Sharon the railings, where I had got my head stuck many years earlier.

There were many other occasions when we went into London, too many to write about, however each visit was great.

Sharon took me on a Showboat Evening cruise along the River Thames, which we both really enjoyed. A three-course meal followed by live music from the West End shows. We also did a similar cruise but this time it was with an Elvis impersonator.

On 27 August 2016, we celebrated our second anniversary of meeting, albeit early, by spending the night in The Tower Hotel, which is situated next to the River Thames and overlooks Tower Bridge and the Tower of London. We also celebrated on the actual anniversary date of 8 September, which I shall talk about later.

Our hotel room was rather posh, with his and her sinks within a marble tiled bathroom, a separate kitchenette with a fully stocked mini bar and another separate room with a leather sofa and small writing desk. We spent the afternoon enjoying the room and relaxing. Later that evening, we had a reservation at the Medieval Banquet Restaurant, which is located in the lovely St Katharine's Dock. This place is so much fun, the waiters and waitresses are dressed in old medieval clothing. There are no knives and forks to eat with, instead you use your hands, and drink soup from bowls. Entertainment involves dancing and games, which both Sharon and I took part in. Drink was flowing all night and I do recall Sharon getting rather merry.

As I have mentioned alcohol, now is a good time to say that I have never drank. I guess this goes back to when I was ill with hepatitis at the age of fourteen; when doctors told me not to drink alcohol for at least two years. As a teenager, I remember people at school getting their hands on any form of alcohol that they could. Whenever there were afterschool parties, they would get rather drunk. I never got involved in this as if I had, it would have made me very ill. Now that I'm an adult, I must say that I am glad that I have never drank, and certainly don't feel that I have missed out at all. I haven't got a problem with anyone who does, but know your limitations and certainly don't drink and drive. When you have seen the devastation that I have seen on our roads, caused by drinking and driving, you can understand why I am so against it.

Like I have already said, we went to London a lot and also said each time was great, but let me just elaborate on that; Sharon and I were lucky enough to visit many places in this country and abroad. One thing which I know is that it's not just about the place; it's about who you are there with, which makes each place special. You can be anywhere in the world, but if you are with the wrong person, that place you are in can soon become tarnished with unhappy memories.

This is probably why I remember everything that I did with Sharon. We were so happy and made so many special memories.

Before I bring this chapter to a close, there is one photo that I would like to share with you. This being Sharon sitting on the lattice bench outside the Bank of England, which I made and fitted when doing my carpentry and joinery apprenticeship, many years ago.

Chapter Twenty
Concerts and Festivals

Remember when I told you earlier about Sharon's Brighton birthday, and that I had got tickets to see Queen. Well, this was our very first concert that we went to, and first time together at the O2 arena in London.

The date was Sunday, 18 January 2015, and as usual we arrived early, which gave us time to walk around the various food outlets. We chose the Chinese Buffet restaurant, which by now was quite busy. We were led to our table, where on this occasion we sat opposite each other. Generally, when Sharon and I went out to restaurants or quaint tearooms, we would sit next to each other, and if need be, rearrange the cutlery and place settings accordingly. This wasn't something which we planned or even spoke about, it just naturally happened. We wanted to be close together, our personal spaces overlapping and becoming one. We finished the meal and decided to load our pockets with the sweets, which were meant for the chocolate fountain. With pockets now bulging, we made our way into the arena. Our seats were overlooking the stage with just the balcony in front of us. Queen, with Adam Lambert, were brilliant, we sang and danced all night. I found out that evening that Sharon's favourite song by Queen is 'Under Pressure', she knew every single word!

It was in June of 2016 that we went to see two concerts, Rod Stewart, and Lionel Richie. The first being on 4 June 2016, which was at Norwich City Football Stadium, where Rod Stewart was playing.

Being as Norwich is a fair way to travel, we decided to turn it into a mini break. So, I booked up a little cottage, with a hot tub, just outside of the city. The weather was again very hot and sunny. We spent two nights here and spent the time relaxing. I drove to the football stadium and managed to find somewhere to park the car, of course we were early so it wasn't too busy. We grabbed some food from a nearby supermarket and found a grassed area outside the stadium, where we tucked into our cooked chicken salad. Once inside the stadium, we made our way to our seats, which were centre of the stage and about twenty rows back. The view of the stage was fantastic from our sitting position, however once

Rod Stewart walked out for his first song, everyone stood up. For the next two hours, we were on our feet dancing. (So much for paying premium rates for good 'seats'). After the concert, we went back to our little cottage and relaxed under the stars in the hot tub. It must have been about 03.00hrs by the time we got into bed. The bed! Well, you know I said the cottage was little; the bed was also little and made from wafer thin wooden struts. I spent the next morning using my carpentry skills repairing it.

On Saturday 25 June 2016, Lionel Ritchie was playing at Colchester Football Stadium, Essex. Which is about a forty-minute drive from our home in Chelmsford. This time we were sitting in the stadium stands, to the left-hand side of the stage, which were undercover, just as well because at one point the rain poured down so hard. We also managed to remain seated most of the time, only getting up to dance on the spot and of course singing along to all the tracks. On the way home, we spoke about the concert, and both agreed that we enjoyed Lionel more than Rod.

It was on 16th July when we rocked at the Lets rock London 80's Festival. This was our first music festival and we really had fun. I had words with one of the security team guarding the posh toilets and showed him my fire brigade ID card. For the whole day and night, Sharon and I were able to use the posh loos, rather than the smelly portable plastic ones. I tried the same two months later, Sunday, 11 September 2016, when we went with my sister Angela and her husband, to the British Summer Time music festival in Hyde Park, London. This time it didn't work.

On the stage, that day was Elton John, Status Quo, Madness and many more.

It was on this day whilst on the train to London that we told Angela about our wedding plans, which you shall read about later.

Another concert that we went to was Robbie Williams at the London Stadium, Stratford. This was on the 23rd June 2017. We were in two minds whether we should go to this concert, because the chemotherapy that Sharon was having at the time made her immune system low, and she was at risk of picking up infections. A couple of days before the concert, I insisted that Sharon have a blood test, to check her white blood cell count. Fortunately, it was a good level, so we were able to go. The Robbie concert was great, however, when it finished, I became concerned, because the route back to the train station was a long way and was packed with others leaving the stadium. Sharon was tired and not up to walking. So, my fire brigade ID made another appearance, and I had words with the security, and we were able to take a short cut back to the station.

Over the four years that I had with Sharon we also went to see many tribute acts at local theatres and at weekend breaks. We loved to sing and dance.

There is also another concert which we went to which I shall tell you about later.

Chapter Twenty-One
My Valentine

This book is about the love that Sharon and I shared. So why have I waited until now to talk about Valentine's Day? My answer to that is, every day with Sharon was special and full of love, and not just for one day, 14 February. We didn't need the excuse of Valentine's Day to say how much we loved each other. This we did every day and as I said at the very start of this book Love is a feeling of happiness and contentment. With that said, we did make Valentine's special for each other.

We celebrated four Valentine's Days together…

Our first Valentine's Day 2015.

The celebrations started on 13 February, when I booked an afternoon tea and evening spa at Greenwoods Hotel and Spa in Stock, just down the road from where Sharon and I first met in that coffee shop. This was the first afternoon tea that Sharon had ever had, and it was to become the first of many. We arrived early, surprisingly enough, which worked in our favour because we had the choice of where we wanted to sit. Sharon chose the soft green leather sofa which was great, because we were able to sit next to each other and it was nice and cosy. The afternoon tea arrived and was placed on a table in front of us along with a selection of teas from around the world. Soft gentle piano music played in the background. Later that evening, we spent time relaxing in the spa, making use of the sauna, steam room and hot tub. The whole experience was so romantic. Sharon stayed with me that night as we had an early start on the next day.

It was around 07.00hrs when we started our journey to Bournemouth, the seaside town in Dorset on the South coast. I had booked a boutique hotel which had a room with a sea view and a balcony. After checking in and having a cuppa in the room, we went for a walk along the sea front, in the direction of the pier. Even though there was a chill in the air, it was sunny at times. We stopped at the memorial for the RAF Red Arrows pilot, who sadly died following a crash at the Bournemouth Air Festival on 20 August 2011. We carried on walking past the pier and into the town centre, where we stopped for a coffee before retracing our steps back to the hotel. I had already booked a romantic Valentine's meal at the hotel restaurant for later that night. The dining room had been decorated with red hearts and sprinkled on the crisp white tablecloths were red sparkly beads. It was after our main meal and whilst waiting for desserts that the 'Flux Capacitor' made an appearance, we laughed so much. Happy memories.

Next day we again walked into the town centre and looked around the shops. We planned to see 'Fifty Shades of Grey' later that day.

What happened next was the beginning of 'The Essex Angels'!

As we walked along, I could see a group of people standing by a car, some were taking photos with their phone. It soon become apparent that there had been a collision involving a car and pedestrians. Nobody was helping the casualties, so Sharon and I went straight to their aid. The car's engine was still running, I asked the driver to turn it off. There was a man with a serious fracture to his lower leg. He was laying on the floor next to the front wheel of the car. His partner had also been hit and had bruising to her legs. My concern was the gentleman's head, he had been involved in a collision and I wasn't sure if he had damaged his spine. I got on the floor with him and held his head still, whilst Sharon supported the man's fractured leg. I explained that Sharon was a health care support worker and that I was an off-duty fire fighter, and that my name was Russell and we were from Essex. An on looker called the emergency services. Sharon and I stayed with both casualties, reassuring them until paramedics arrived. The lady was clearly very upset as she watched the paramedics straighten her partner's damaged leg and move him to the back of the ambulance. Sharon comforted her and even got her a drink from a nearby coffee shop. We then left the scene and went to a nearby Italian Restaurant for dinner, by now we were both rather hungry. We briefly spoke about what had happened and hoped that they would make a full recovery. Then we went to watch the movie at the cinema, it was funny because I was the only man there. I was surrounded by women watching scenes involving whipping and tying up, if only I could have read their minds. I reckon I have a good idea what they were thinking. Probably the same as me, how rubbish the acting was!

It wasn't until the 11 March 2015 when Sharon's friend called her, to say that there was an article in the local Essex Chronicle Newspaper. I went out to the local newsagents and bought a copy:

CRASH VICTIMS IN SEARCH FOR THEIR ESSEX ANGELS.

A couple hurt in a road accident are looking for 'Essex Angels' who looked after them until paramedics arrived. Karen Green, 56 and Garry Tom Taylor, 60, from London and Bournemouth respectively, were enjoying a Valentine's weekend in Bournemouth when they were knocked over in the town centre on Sunday 15th February at 3pm.

But two bystanders from Essex, a nurse and a fireman, who were also enjoying a romantic weekend away, came to their aid, keeping them calm and looking after them while the ambulance was on its way.

Ms Green, a mother of one, said: "We had been shopping in the town, and were crossing the road at about 3pm when a taxi ploughed into us.

The car actually stopped on my legs, and I screamed for the driver to move forward, which luckily, she did. Two people rushed over, they turned out to be a fireman and a nurse. The nurse looked after me while the fireman knelt in the road and held Garry's head until the ambulance came.

As soon as the paramedics arrived, he asked one of them to take over as he had been stuck in one position making sure Garry's head and back were OK, as we didn't know what the injuries were at the time."

And the couple are so desperate to thank the Essex good Samaritans that they wrote to the mayor's office at Chelmsford City Council, asking staff there to pass on details to the Chronicle in hope that the readers could locate the pair.

"They did not hesitate in coming forward when so many people just stopped and took photographs," said Garry, a former army Captain, in his letter to the council.

"If all people who live in Essex are of this calibre, then you are a very lucky mayor."

The couple were taken to Poole Hospital, where Captain Taylor was treated for a broken ankle, which needed an operation, while Ms Green was lucky her legs weren't broken, although they are currently too badly damaged for her to be able to return to work.

The Mayor of Chelmsford, Councillor Bob Villa said, "It's always lovely to hear of those willing to help others in times of need. The mayoress and I are very keen to help Captain Taylor and his partner track down the Essex couple who assisted them in Bournemouth over the Valentine's weekend.

I'm hoping that a joint effort between officers here at Chelmsford City Council and the Chronicle, their plea will be seen by the 'unsung heroes' and they can be reunited once again.

I hope that Captain Taylor recovers well and is able to return home soon."

Ms Green added, "We just want to be able to thank them for what they did, at least write a letter to them. They were so kind. When I was talking to the nurse, she said they were down in Bournemouth for a romantic weekend and that they were from Essex."

Ms Green added. "They were like angels; they just appeared and helped out. The nurse even got me a cup of tea while she was looking after me."

"We chatted a bit about our romantic weekends and she told me they were staying in one of the hotels nearby and were planning of seeing 50 Shades of Grey in the afternoon."

On the next page is a photo of that news story…

Crash victims in search for their 'Essex Angels'

Couple want to find 'good Samaritans'

By Harriet Sinclair

ROMANTIC WEEKEND: Karen Green and her partner Gerry Tom Taylor

Sharon contacted The Essex Chronicle and said that we were the people that they were looking for. Next, we had the newspaper photographers and journalist coming to my house to ask questions. A follow up story was published, and it also made the London Evening Standard.

I did contact the former army Captain by phone, and he personally thanked us. I have since changed phones and no longer have his number. I hope he and his partner are keeping well, and if he ever reads this book, I hope that he will remember the other part of The Essex Angels. Whom herself is now an Angel, watching over all of us.

Recently I was looking at my phone and decided to do a 'Google' search of our names Sharon Tucker (Sharon's previous name) and Russell Webb, to my surprise the story is actually there along with a photo of Sharon and myself, taken at City Hall in London, whilst at a Fire Brigade awards ceremony.

Valentines 2016...

By now, we were living together and, on 14 February 2016, Sharon made a special three course meal for us. She prepared the table with red velvet heart shaped table mats and lit tea light candles, it looked amazing and the meal she cooked was far better than any restaurant meal. The following day we went into London to see a show and we stayed overnight in a hotel, which had a swimming pool in the basement.

Valentines 2017...

I was on duty on 14 February 2017, day shift. That night when I got home from work, we had a takeaway meal. Our celebrations began on Friday the 17th, when we went away for a few days to the Warner Leisure Cricket St Thomas Hotel, which is in Somerset. It was a full weekend of live music, featuring various tribute acts which were brilliant. On the Sunday, we visited Cheddar Gorge, took a sightseeing open top bus tour and visited the caves where the Cheddar cheese is stored. Sharon by now was having chemotherapy and was fatigued. However, she still managed to climb the steps, known as Jacob's ladder, right to the top where there is a lookout tower, a total of 274 steps in all. Sharon was physically exhausted, we stopped a few times, but she was determined to do it.

On the Monday, we travelled to Southampton, stopping off at Bournemouth along the way, for a stroll along the beach. In Southampton, we went to see the show, Billy Elliot. We stayed overnight and travelled home the next day.

Valentine 2018.

This was our first Valentine's as husband and wife. We went into London and had afternoon tea in a posh hotel, this was a wedding present from one of Sharon's work friends. In the evening, we went to the West End to see a show. Little did I know that this was also going to be our last ever Valentine's Day!

Chapter Twenty-Two
Scotland Road Trip

It was 16 March 2015 at 11.30hrs that our trip commenced, I know the exact time because I took a short video of us in the car as we were about to set off. My Volvo V70 estate car was packed full, with clothing for all types of weather, camping chairs and blankets. As well as a portable camping gas cooker, stainless steel flask filled with steaming hot water and our 12 volts plug-in blue cool box that we called the fridge. Inside this, there was milk, bacon, sausages and small cubes of butter which were kindly donated by the NHS, from the kitchen on Sharon's ward!

This road trip wasn't done at random; we had carefully planned it, working out travel times between each place we visited. I printed out an A4 size itinerary, with dates and addresses of the hotels and bed and breakfasts that we were staying in. Sharon wrote things on this as we went from place to place. I've not seen this itinerary since we came home, and I can only assume that Sharon has put it in her memory box. About a month before our trip Sharon bought her first ever pair of size 6 hiking boots and a waterproof coat, which had a detachable fleece lining. We would go out for walks where I lived, so that Sharon could break her new boots in. I remember Sharon telling me about someone that she knew who had made fun of her by saying, "Since you have been with Russ, you have really changed; you would have never gone walking or been seen wearing hiking boots."

As we started wearing our boots more and more and going on different adventures, our boots became known as our *invincibles,* because we could cross any terrain without getting sore or wet feet. Today Sharon's boots which actually seemed to have moulded to the shape of her feet, sit next to mine on a shelf in my outbuilding, a pair of thick socks last worn by Sharon are tucked inside. I have since bought myself a new pair of hiking boots. The *invincibles* shall remain together for always.

Our first stop was at a spa hotel which Sharon had booked, situated just on the edge of the Peak District. On route, we managed to find a beautiful picnic area within woodlands. Here we got the cooker out and we had bacon and sausages in crusty rolls, which were probably the best bacon rolls I have ever had.

Whilst we were in the Peak District, we spent the day at Chatsworth House and enjoyed walking around the surrounding countryside.

Next stop was the Lake District, where we spent the night in a hotel positioned right on the edge of Lake Windermere. We arrived early but couldn't check in straight away, so we went and sat on the hotel's private pontoon and enjoyed a cuppa from the flask, whilst taking in the stunning scenery. Our room was more like an apartment which had its own patio area which overlooked the lake.

The next day we explored the lake from the top deck of a tour boat, the weather was sunny with no clouds in the sky. This boat tour lasted about an hour and half, it was so peaceful and relaxing. Being as it was out of season, there weren't many tourists around, which made it feel like it was just us visiting this beautiful area.

Our road trip continued travelling northwards avoiding motorways and dual carriage ways wherever I could. My satellite navigation system does seem to avoid these routes anyway, maybe I have set it up wrong. On many other trips, Sharon always joked about how we would end up travelling down the narrowest country lanes or even a dirt track through the middle of a farmer's field.

Our next stop was Helensburgh on the west coast of Scotland, which is north of Glasgow. It was on the next day 20 March 2015 that we witnessed a total eclipse of the sun. We stood on our balcony with a mug of tea and felt a sudden drop in the temperature and an eerie silence as the sun hid behind the moon. We didn't spend much time here as it was just a quick overnight stop.

We carried on heading north, this time our destination was Fort Augustus, which is at the bottom edge of Loch Ness. The scenery as you drive through the highlands is amazing, we stopped at a layby at the side of the road, where we set up a shelter using travel rugs draped between the rear and front car doors. The camping chairs came out as did the camping stove and we had our very first roadside omelette and of course, a hot mug of tea from the flask. The air is fresh and the coldness as you breathe it in hurts your nostrils. In the distance, snow-capped mountains stand tall, whilst the lower ridges desperately cling on to their last white blanket before turning into icy streams. This was really a special place.

We reached Fort Augustus in the late afternoon and checked into our hotel which overlooked Loch Ness. After relaxing for a while and taking a shower, we walked down to the Loch and sat on the edge of a pontoon. Leaning forwards slightly, we watched our reflections in the dark still water, we didn't talk we just sat and watched. Every now and then a gentle breeze would distort our reflections and we would smile and laugh. In the evening, we stopped at a pub next to the five locks, which forms part of the Caledonian Canal. Inside the quaint little pub an open fire burns, the smell of the logs smouldering lingers in the air, and flickering candles in old wine bottles stand on tables. It was in this pub where we had the best fish and chips meal ever. The fish had been freshly caught that morning; it was pure white in colour. The beer batter was crispy, and the chips were proper chunky.

One day I will go back to Loch Ness and sit on the same pontoon; just maybe I will see the reflection of my lovely wife.

Next day we checked out and took the road which runs next to Loch Ness and headed to Inverness. We stopped here for a coffee before beginning our journey back southwards.

Our next stop was a bed and breakfast in a village on the edge of Hadrian's Wall. Our room was in a converted stable on a working farm, which had uninterrupted countryside views, which were stunning. That night the farmer took us into one of the barns to show us the sheep, it was lambing season, so we were lucky enough to see a lamb born. The breakfast next morning was delicious, all fresh produce and freshly baked bread with a selection of homemade jams and marmalades.

As we headed south our final stop was in Scarborough on the east coast of England. Whilst here we visited the famous Robin Hoods Bay, a small fishing village leading down to the North Sea. We stayed in this area for a couple of nights and sat on the beach at Whitby, where the seagulls are massive.

Now most people I speak to say that once the holiday is over, they just want to get home as quickly as possible. Well in our case we always made the journey home just as enjoyable by stopping off at different locations. So, on the way home from Scarborough, we stopped at some lovely beaches and were able to get the camping stove out and have a hot bacon roll. We also drove through some pretty villages and if my memory serves me right, we even stopped for a cream tea in a little tearoom.

Chapter Twenty-Three
Time at Home

As I am putting pen to paper and reading over the chapters, I am aware that to some of you, it may be like reading a travel guide. However, I like to think of it as a journey. The journey of two people who were searching for love and found each other, two people who just wanted to live and enjoy every second together be it at home, going shopping, mini breaks, or holidays abroad. For Sharon and me, making memories was so important. Looking back now it is as though someone or something was guiding us and telling us to make the most of everything that we did. In the four years, I had with Sharon we were lucky to travel to many places and make special memories that I will cherish forever. I often look back at the many photos and videos that I took and for a moment I am once again reliving those wonderful times. Sadly, there are also photos which I took when Sharon was very poorly, and as much as I try to forget those not so nice memories, they will always be there to haunt me.

It's now April 2015 and we have been back from the road trip about a week. One of the hardest things after spending times together, was having to say bye to each other afterwards, remember Sharon was still living in Chelmsford. We managed to see each other at least two to three times a week, grabbing every opportunity that we could to be together, in-between our work and family life.

When we weren't travelling, Sharon would stay over at my house and we would spend our time going out for days or walking around my local area. We would spend time in my garden with the fire pit alight relaxing, sometimes we had music playing. There were also times when we just sat and listened to the crackles from the fire and to the sounds of the night time wildlife. And of course, on clear nights we would put the king-size blow-up bed out on the lawn and stargaze. Sharon told me that she would often stay up late and struggled to fall asleep straight away. Whenever she would stay over with me, I would play relaxing music by Kenny G, the saxophonist, and Sharon would snuggle into my chest while I stroked the side of her face and ran my fingers through her hair. It didn't take too long for her to drift off.

It's now the end of May 2015 and we were planning our first holiday abroad; I must say, Sharon was very good with finding a bargain. One evening we sat down after dinner and began to surf the internet holiday sites and around an hour later, we found a five-star resort in Sharm El-Sheik, Egypt. We booked our holiday for the first two weeks in July, but before then we had a mini break in Norfolk in mid-June, which Sharon had booked for my valentine's gift from her. We stayed in a cabin with its own hot tub sunken into the decking. These few days away were so relaxing and yet again we were so lucky with the weather. On one day, we walked through the wheat fields and found a hidden stream, where we stopped and had a picnic, not a sound could be heard, except for the birds in the trees and the water slowly trickling over decaying branches. In the evenings as the sun was setting, we relaxed in the hot tub, wine for Sharon and orange juice for me.

Our holiday in Egypt in July 2015 was wonderful, the resort we stayed on was huge, we ate in a different restaurant every night. The daytime temperature was very hot, we kept cool by going in and out of the sea, and it was here that Sharon first tried snorkelling. I had taken my masks and snorkels with me because I had read the reviews about the many species of fish that could be seen at the end of the long wooden jetty. It was whilst I was getting out of the water and back onto the stairs of the jetty, that a wave pushed me into the steps, and I cut my ankle. It wasn't a deep cut, but it did scar me and whenever I look down at my ankle, I am reminded of that time that we first went snorkelling together.

We got home from our first holiday abroad on 12 July 2015. Two days later we were on another mini break, this time we were in Bath and stayed in a charming bed and breakfast about twenty minutes from the city. The first day we visited Longleat safari park, we had so much fun here especially as you drove through the monkey enclosure. Here the little primates jump onto your car and hitch a free ride, they have been known to cause a lot of damage to cars. We had a lucky escape because they seemed more interested in looking at themselves in the door mirrors. There is another area where you can feed the deer from your vehicles, as you drive through their enclosure. The funniest thing happened, Sharon was holding a cup with the deer food in it then all of a sudden, this deer stuck her head into the car through the open window and nuzzled her wet nose into the cup of food which happened to be on Sharon's lap. That day Sharon was wearing a skirt and as you would imagine the skirt was pushed up as the deer tucked in, searching for every last pellet of food. I captured the moment on video and later Sharon uploaded it on YouTube; *'OH DEER ME, HOW VERY RUDE!'* *by Sharon Tucker.* It makes me laugh each time I watch it.

The next day we went to Bath and took an open top bus ride around the city, taking in the ancient sites.

We had a brilliant time in Longleat and in Bath, so much that Sharon really wanted to return with her daughter and grandson. We were able to go back with them at the end of July 2018, thanks to a local charity, which I shall talk about later.

In the August of 2015, we went camping with my children, Jason and Mia and their partners at that time. The place we went to was on the Dorset Coast near Bridport, a lovely family run camping and caravan site called Freshwater Bay.

My tent is rather large, and I can stand up in it and with the addition of a fitted carpet in the lounge area, electric hook up for lighting and heating it's like a home from home. It was lovely being away with Sharon and my children, she really got on well with them and both Jason and Mia were very fond of her.

I have lovely memories of our time camping but one which sticks in my mind is the night that we all went down to the beach; it was pitch black and the only light was from the stars above. We took some Chinese lanterns away with us, and that night was the perfect time to send them up into the night sky. The idea of these lanterns is they are made of thin paper in a hot air balloon shape, with a rigid twisted paper ring at the bottom supporting a flammable wadding; the size of these ones were roughly two feet tall and eighteen inches in circumference. You set alight some wadding which heats up the air within the lantern and it rises up. Well, our first attempt crash landed on the beach and the whole thing went up in flames, the second attempt the strings holding the wadding burnt away. But the third and fourth ones were great, as they slowly filled with hot air and began to rise, we all cheered and clapped, our eyes fixated on the flickering lanterns as they climbed higher and higher into the night time darkness.

Chapter Twenty-Four
Proposal Plans

It wasn't long after meeting Sharon, that I realised that I wanted to spend the rest of my life with her. There was a connection and a special bond between us. I wanted to have the honour of being her husband.

It was whilst we were in the bed and breakfast on our trip to Longleat and Bath that the plans began.

I have always wanted to visit New York, so I asked Sharon if she fancied a trip to the Big Apple later that year. I said that it would be an early birthday present from me. After searching flights and hotels, I pressed the confirm booking button on my phone and paid the deposit.

The stage was set, New York was to be where I would propose. The question was how I was going to do it? When would I do it? The first thing was to totally steer her off the track; as Sharon was still legally married, I said to her that I would never want to get engaged whilst she still had that connection, and that I felt very strongly about it.

Back in February 2015, whilst we were in Bournemouth, we were having a coffee in a cafe which overlooked the sea. I was messing about with the empty sugar sachets again and made a makeshift ring, which I placed on Sharon's wedding ring finger, twisting the edges together to resemble a diamond. After a while, Sharon took it off and left it on the table, as we were leaving the cafe, I discreetly picked it up and placed it in my wallet. This was the ring gauge that I used to get her size. In early August 2015, I took my sugar sachet gauge into a jeweller's, got it sized and went shopping for a ring. (I can suddenly hear the voices of a thousand women reading this saying "NO! let the woman choose her own ring"). Well, this couldn't be because it had to be a total surprise. I chose a white gold ring with four diamonds in a square cluster, which had four smaller diamonds each side set into the band. At the same time, I bought an eternity ring in white gold with diamonds running around 50% of the band, which complimented the engagement ring when put together. My plan was to give this to Sharon at Christmas time which I shall talk about later.

In the background whilst I was making plans, a lot was happening; Sharon had sold her home which she had lived in for twenty-seven years with her husband and children. The moving date was 27 August 2015, I helped move the contents of the house into a storage unit nearby. Sharon moved in with me whilst we looked for a new home together.

We had our first anniversary of meeting each other on 8 September 2015, when we went back to the same coffee shop in Stock and then went onto Southend, where we sat on "Sharon and Russell's" bench eating a Rossi ice cream. We said that we would always relive our first date by doing the same thing each year, which we did in 2016, however in 2017 we were in Fuerteventura. Nowadays, since Sharon's passing; each year on 8 September, I go to that coffee shop, then head to Southend and walk in the same direction as we did, I stop and get an ice cream and sit on our bench. I leave a bunch of flowers tucked between the wooden slats where my lovely wife once sat. I always leave some ice cream in the bottom of the cornet and place it in the bushes behind for Sharon. I sit here for ages just looking taking in the same views as we did together. I just don't speak to Sharon; we have conversations and as strange as this may seem to some, I do hear her voice and hear her laugh. Not just here on our bench but everywhere.

Taken 8 September 2015

Taken 8 September 2016

Taken 8 September 2018

We eventually found our first home together, a rented four-bedroom detached house in Writtle, Chelmsford. On 10 September 2015, I hired another lorry and with the help of family and friends we moved Sharon's items from the storage and into our new home. The sad thing was I couldn't move in straight away as I was still in contract with my rented home. It wasn't to be until we came back from New York in November 2015 that we would officially share our first home together.

Our first home, moving day, 10 September 2015

Chapter Twenty-Five
The West Country

Before I talk about New York and reveal the wedding proposal, I want to tell you about our adventures in Devon.

It was in October 2015, that we first went to Devon, we stayed in a self-catering bungalow at Harcombe House, owned and run by The Firefighters Charity.

Let me tell you about the charity first; it has three centres. One in Devon, one in Penrith and the other on the south coast at Littlehampton. In their words, *"The Firefighters Charity offers specialist, lifelong support for members of the UK fire services community, empowering individuals to achieve mental, physical and social wellbeing throughout their lives."* Help and advice is also available online or over the phone. I have used the charity on a few occasions prior to meeting Sharon. I had an accident at work and injured my knee which required physiotherapy. I attended two of the centres and was put on a week-long physiotherapy course which helped strengthen my knee and helped with my recovery. The first time that the charity helped me was back in July 1999; when I stayed at Harcombe House for recuperation with Tina, my first wife, and our children.

At the Harcombe House site in Chudleigh, Devon, there are several bungalows which can be rented out as a holiday let, any fees paid go straight back into the charity. Members of the firefighting community can also stay here free of charge, for recuperation and whilst they on a physio or well-being course.

In the October 2015 visit, we rented a bungalow for a week, and yet again the weather was wonderful. Harcombe House is positioned within three hundred acres of woodland with fishing lakes surrounded by rolling hills. We would often go for a walk down to the lakes and up into the woods and here is my description of one of our walks:

As we step out of our bungalow, the air feels clean and fresh, the sound of cows can be heard in a nearby field. Our walk takes us down the hill and past a memorial. We stop here for a while and I explain to Sharon, that the memorial is for the first female firefighter, in peace time, who tragically lost her life whilst fighting a fire in a supermarket on 4 February 1996. We continue down the tarmac track, with neatly cut hedgerows to each side, about halfway down there is a gate, big enough for a farmer's tractor to fit through, the view down the valley from here is outstanding. Once at the bottom, the tarmac disappears making way for a traditional dirt track, here we turn right and in front of us is one of the lakes. Sunlight peering through the tall trees, reflecting golden sparkles on the surface. We can hear birds singing and the sound of water gently making its way down to a lower-level lake. Hand in hand we stroll around the lake, crossing over the dirt track near the bridge, to our right is a woodman's hut with logs stacked high, the smell of freshly cut timber clings in the air. Over the track, we continue following the path of the stream, a tall rustic picnic table made from the trunk of a tree stands close by. The flow of water here speeds up as the stream is met by the waters from another lake higher up. We sit here for a while, listening to the sounds and watching. Next, we head up some log steps cut into the muddy slope, which now takes us away from the lakes and up amongst the trees. At the top, we stop for a drink of water before continuing up the gentle slope taking us high up into the woods. This walk eventually takes us past the perimeter white fencing of Exeter Racecourse, there are horses racing today. We are now making our way back towards the bungalow along a tree lined country lane. The leaves are beginning to fall, we stop briefly at the side of the road and sit on an earth mound, we laugh and joke as we throw the dried-up leaves over each other, like wedding confetti. The sun rays shining through the trees makes this moment feel so magical.

Whilst in Devon we used the bungalow as a base and went out exploring different areas. It was in Dartmouth sitting in the old railway cafe which overlooks the river that we had our first proper cream tea. Warm scones, strawberry jam with clotted cream. In Torquay, a boat trip took us around the bay. It seemed that wherever Sharon and I went we would try to fit in a boat trip, be it on the sea or inland on a canal or river.

On one of the days, we drove across the county to North Devon and went to the beautiful fishing village called Clovelly. To get down to the harbour you walk down steep narrow cobbled stone streets which twist and turn, pretty cottages all with their own charm and character stand on each side. Sharon had never been here before and she absolutely fell in love with this quaint little village.

Clovelly, 12 October 2015

In August 2016, we went on holiday again with Jason and Mia and stayed in one of the bungalows at Harcombe House.

One evening we decided to go to the seaside town of Teignmouth, we were armed with camping chairs, blankets, the cool box with food and drink as well as charcoal and a grille from the bungalow oven which we borrowed! Jason and I dug a shallow hole in the red coloured sand whilst the girls went off collecting pebbles, to lay in the bottom and around the edges. The charcoal was lit, and the grille placed on top, it didn't take too long for the coals to turn white hot, and soon we were eating chicken kebabs, burgers, and sausages. After dinner, we kept the fire alight with small pieces of wood and twigs which had washed up in the tide earlier that day and had dried out in the sun. We had so much fun that night, I reckon it must have been around midnight before our little beach party came to an end.

On another day, we spent the time sitting on the beach at Blackpool Sands, Devon. (Not to be confused with the Blackpool in Lancashire). This beach is a natural horseshoe shaped bay with crystal clear water and today it was a glorious sunny day. Sharon and I decided to go for a walk on our own around the bay, feeling the sand between our toes with the waves gently breaking around our ankles. We found a hidden cove, nobody was there, just us. For a while, we sat where the sand meets the sea with our legs getting wet and our arms stretched out behind us, and our hands were naturally touching each other in the sand.

Nearby, some rocks were emerging from the sea and it was here that I took a photo of Sharon. I have already mentioned that I took many photos of Sharon and selfies in the four years, and have no favourites, to me every single one is special. However, there are some which really do capture the moment, this being one of those.

It was in July 2017 that Sharon and I came back to Devon and stayed again in a bungalow at Harcombe House, this time we were on a week's recuperation, funded by The Firefighters Charity. Sharon had finished her chemotherapy and radiotherapy treatment earlier that month, and was exhausted. To be truthful I was also shattered and needed a break. During our stay we didn't go for long walks up into the woods, we generally drove around the county, visiting places and relaxing. We did however go on a return steam train ride from Buckfastleigh to Totnes, and while we were there Sharon removed her chemo hat for the first time in public. Her hair had now begun to grow back. We also went into Dartmoor national park and set up our camping chairs and camping stove, and had lunch overlooking the beautiful scenery.

Later that week Sharon's daughter and grandson joined us for a few days. Sharon had enjoyed Devon so much previously that she wanted to replicate some of the things we had done with her family. We had another BBQ on the beach in Teignmouth, and on the last day we visited Woolacombe and then went to Clovelly. Remember earlier that I said how steep the cobbled streets are, well I was concerned that it would be difficult for Sharon to walk back up. There is, however, a Land-Rover service near to the harbour, which takes another route back up to the car park. This was mainly for people who would find the walk back up hard going. I was quite expecting Sharon to use this facility; I was so wrong that day. She totally amazed me by walking back up along those steep, drawn-out cobbles. We took it nice and slow and rested when needed. When we reached the top, Sharon was so pleased that she had managed to do it, I was so proud of her.

The final time that Sharon would stay in Devon was in June 2018. We were again on recuperation and staying in the two bungalows with Sharon's children and grandchildren. Sharon really wanted to have this holiday with her family and was really looking forward to it, I'm so happy that with the help of The Firefighters Charity we were able to go. We had another beach party and BBQ on Teignmouth beach and spent another day on the beach at Woolacombe, playing in the sand and swimming in the sea. We did also go to Clovelly again, but this time Sharon and I had a picnic on the grass near the car park whilst the rest of the family went to explore the village. I felt so sad for Sharon, I knew she desperately wanted to experience it again with her family.

I returned to Harcombe House in May 2019 with my son Jason, for a week's recuperation. The first part of the holiday I wanted to retrace the steps that Sharon and I had taken on previous stays, which was very emotional. The second part of the week we went to new places that we hadn't been before. Spending time with Jason was nice and it was also good for us to reflect on the things that had happened. Things which you shall read about later.

Chapter Twenty-Six
The Proposal

Taking you back to 2015, the stage was set, the place was to be New York and my cover story was sorted; we were going there as a gift from me; to celebrate Sharon's birthday. The flights were booked, as was the hotel, and I had the engagement ring well-hidden at home. I just needed a plan. How was I going to pop that all important question? I turned to the internet for some inspiration and started to watch New York Wedding proposals. I spent some time looking at flash mob proposals in Times Square, a romantic proposal on Bow Bridge in Central Park to even a proposal at the top of the Empire State Building. After what seemed like hours, I turned the laptop off and decided to think of my own plan.

First, I thought about taking Sharon to see a show on Broadway, then during the interval I would say I was going to the toilet but really, I would be making my way to the stage and would ask the question in front of everyone.

Next, I found out that the rock singer, Meatloaf, was playing at Madison Square Garden whilst we were there. I could contact his agent and arrange for him to call us both up on stage during his set, where I would pop the question.

Both these ideas soon became null and void, I really wanted it to be more intimate with just Sharon and me. It must have taken about three weeks for my plan to be completed.

Sharon had once told me that her mum would often speak about the Statue of Liberty, and that she always wanted to go there. Unfortunately, Sharon's mum was unwell and was suffering from Dementia, therefore travelling a long distance on a plane would be too stressful for her. So, I thought how nice it would be for her to be able to see photos of her daughter next to the Statue. This was now my chosen place; where I would ask Sharon to marry me, but still I wanted it to be just the two of us.

Liberty Island, where the Statue stands is generally packed with tourists.

Back to the internet; where I found an evening dinner cruise along the Hudson River. So, next day I phoned the cruise company in New York. I explained to the kind lady on the phone that I was going to propose, and that I wanted a good window seat and wanted it to be extra special. She said that all would be taken care of, all I had to do was make myself known to the server as soon as we boarded.

About a week before we were due to fly, I hired a tuxedo with all the trimmings; shiny shoes, crisp white shirt and bow tie. I asked Sharon to pack an evening dress as we were going out for an early birthday meal whilst we were in New York.

On the 8th November 2015, we stayed overnight in a hotel near Gatwick Airport, we were so excited. Next morning, as we were going through security at the airport, I was so nervous. I had the ring packed in my hand luggage; I didn't want it in the hold luggage, just in case it went missing. As I put my travel case on the x-ray machine conveyor belt, I had beads of sweat appearing on my forehead; I must have looked like a drug smuggler!

Would the security see the small square box hidden deep inside or would they just want to do a random search? If so, they would have found the ring and Sharon would have seen it, and the whole plan would have fallen flat on its face before we even took off. Luckily it didn't happen, we passed through security with no problems and silently I breathed a sigh of relief. Our flight left the runway around 08.30hrs.

We arrived in New York around midday Eastern United States time, which is five hours behind the UK time. A private taxi which I had booked was there waiting for us which took us straight to our hotel. The hotel that I chose was two blocks down from the Empire State Building, and next to 5th Avenue. After taking a shower and unpacking our clothes, we ventured out into the streets of New York.

Times Square 9th November 2015

Daylight was just beginning to fade when we reached Times Square, we climbed up a set of red glass steps in the middle of the square which led to nowhere, at the top we stopped and took photos and just listened. There is something about the sound of New York which we often spoke about and I certainly will never forget; the constant noise of traffic, horns beeping, people talking, shouting, sometimes screaming and sirens from police cars and fire appliances. And that noise is twenty-four hours a day and during the early hours, there is the added sound of refuse collections and deliveries being made to the various bars and food outlets. Now I understand what is meant by the saying; "The city that never sleeps."

We picked up our New York passes which we had purchased online a few weeks earlier, these turned out to be really worth the money as they allowed us entry into many of the attractions and more, and we could even go straight to the front of any queues. That first night we managed to have a meal, visit Madam Tussauds wax works museum and go on The Ride, a seventy-five-minute interactive tour and show of Midtown Manhattan and Times Square in a custom-built theatre bus. It must have been around 02.00hrs (7am UK time) when we eventually got into bed, we were shattered and had been awake for twenty-six hours.

The next day 10th November 2015 was the day that I would ask Sharon to be my wife, however, first we had a day of sightseeing to do. We got on the subway (underground train) and made our way to the 911 World Trade Centre Memorial. As we got closer to ground zero, we passed the FDNY, Ten House fire station, where we stopped for a while and paid our respects. Whilst we were there, they picked up an emergency call to One World Trade Centre, the new sky scraper reaching high up into the clear blue sky. It was quite poignant watching the fire fighters turn out in their shiny chromed turn table ladder appliance, brightly decorated with stars and stripes, and two USA flags attached to the rear which blew in the wind. Thankfully this time it was a false alarm and after around twenty minutes they were back at the fire house.

Even though I am a fire fighter myself, I find it difficult to imagine what must have gone through those fire fighters' heads on that fateful day, 11 September 2001. I have the upmost respect for those fire fighters and other emergency workers who sadly lost their lives that day, and for those who have lost their lives since the attacks, as a result of illnesses brought on by exposure to the dust.

Standing next to the square memorial fountains, which are on the same footprint as the original World Trade Centre buildings, and hearing the sound of the water falling into the centre pools, makes the hairs on the back of my neck stand up. We slowly walk around each fountain stopping occasionally to read some of the names of the people who perished.

The museum is tastefully done and very emotional, we spent all morning here looking at the displays and reading the news articles.

We arrived back at our hotel around 15.00hrs and were both shattered, so we laid on the bed for a while and nodded off for a couple of hours. At 19.00hrs, we were ready and went down into the lobby, to wait for a cab which I had booked. Whilst we were waiting, I asked a hotel porter to take a photo of us. Sharon looked stunning as she always did. I was wearing the suit that I had hired. The ring was in a box wrapped in my handkerchief to conceal the shape and I had it in my right-hand jacket pocket. Now, the reason it was in this pocket was I was thinking that; I always hold Sharon's right hand in my left hand and if I were to put my arm around her, she would be unable to feel the bulge in my pocket. I was very aware of the ring and was so worried that it may be seen or worse still, I could lose it.

By now, Sharon knew that we were going on an evening dinner cruise for her birthday and whilst we were waiting for the cab, she made a post on her Facebook.

On the next page is a screenshot of the photo and comment that Sharon posted that night.

My very own James Bond!!! Just about to go
for a birthday dinner cruise...cant wait xxxx

We arrived at the Chelsea Piers and as we stepped onto the jetty, we could see our ship, it was very long with full length windows which reflected the twinkling lights of the surrounding buildings and live piano music could be heard as we got closer. A smartly dressed lady greeted us at the reception desk and took our names, another lady showed us to our table and said that our server would be along shortly. When I telephoned the cruise and booked it a few weeks earlier, I had asked for our table to be in a good spot and for six long stem roses to be placed on the table. Sure enough, the roses were there along with a bottle of Champagne and a gift bag containing two Champagne flutes. Our table was positioned near to the rear of the ship and in the corner next to the windows, the perfect spot, we could see the live band and had panoramic views through the crystal-clear windows which curved at the top and continued above our heads.

Our server introduced himself whilst passing us the menus and wished Sharon a Happy Birthday and said that he was going to make it really special for her. We left the pier and began cruising along the Hudson and East rivers, past the skyscrapers of Manhattan. We were able to go out on the rear deck, it was windy and there was a drizzle in the air, the atmosphere was amazing, and as we went under Brooklyn Bridge, everyone cheered. The meal was very posh indeed and we both really enjoyed it. All the time I was thinking to myself, *Where and when would we get to the Statue of Liberty.*

On a toilet break, our server followed me into the gents, reassuring me that he knew all about my proposal plans, and that he would come and let me know once we were getting close to the Statue.

We were back at our table having a drink and talking; when our server came over and said that because it was a special occasion, Sharon's birthday, he had spoken with the captain of the ship, who gave us permission to go to the top of the ship, next to the bridge, where we had our own private viewing deck. He led us up a narrow staircase to the ship's bridge and then onto a small deck, he said we could stay there for a while and enjoy the close-up views of the Statue of Liberty.

So, there we were, just the two of us, on our own private deck with nobody around us. The ship's engines had stopped and it was peaceful and quiet. Sharon had her back to me and was taking photos and it was then that I noticed the ship's photographer, crouching behind the container of an inflatable life raft.

It was at this point that I removed the box from my pocket and got down on one knee. Now, I had planned ahead and knew that it would be dark, so I purchased a box with a built-in light, which shines a bright light directly on the ring once the box is opened.

Sharon was busy clicking away when I said 'Sharon', which was strange of me because I never called her by her name, generally I would say, 'Darling'. Sharon turned around and I said these words, "Sharon my Darling I love you so much, will you marry me." Her response was overwhelming, she had tears rolling down her cheeks and the biggest smile ever. By now, I was back on my feet, the photographer was taking photos, the ring was sparkling in the light from the box. Sharon's reply was 'yes, yes, yes'.

I took the ring from the box and placed it on her finger and slowly pushed it on, it fitted perfectly.

The photographer congratulated us and handed us both a glass of Champagne, she took a few more photos and then left us to enjoy the moment alone.

I took the photo on the next page; it needs no title because it captures every beautiful emotion. I have had it enlarged and it is now on my living room wall.

We stayed on our own private deck for a while, holding each other. It was a wonderful moment which is difficult to put into words, so just take a look at the photo on the following page and you can almost feel the love emanating.

We made our way back down the narrow staircase and back into the main seating area, it was then that the captain announced our engagement over the ship's public address system. Everyone cheered and clapped; women came forward and hugged Sharon and wanted to look at her ring, men shook my hand and patted me on the back. The walk back to our table was like running the gauntlet, in a nice way of course.

For the rest of the night, Sharon kept looking down at her ring and yes, you guessed right, I had to take a photo.

So, mainly for the ladies reading this, I promised that I would show you Sharon's engagement ring.

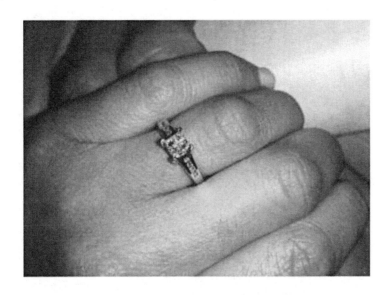

Next morning, we sat in the hotel's lobby area, drinking coffee while we made use of their free wi-fi. Sharon made calls to her family and friends to give them the good news. I also rang my family who already knew that I was going to propose. It was 11th November 2015 and similar to the UK, which has Remembrance Day, in the United States they have Veterans' Day, and there happened to be a carnival procession through New York, which passed right near to our hotel. We stood at the corner of the street and watched the parade. Motor bikes and choppers led the way followed by vintage police cars. Military personnel, both serving and veterans walked in their respective uniforms, some were being pushed in wheel chairs; a visual reminder of the traumas that they must have suffered.

In the afternoon, we wanted to see the Statue of Liberty in day light, so we got the ferry across to the Island. We were unable to go inside the statue and climb up to the torch, I had tried three weeks earlier to book this, but there was no availability. We still walked around the base of the statue and looked across the water to see the Manhattan skyline.

This may sound strange, but even though there were many other tourists, it felt like it was just us. We both talked about this and both said that when looking at each other we only see us. Nobody else in our line of vision matters so sub consciously we blank them out, and it's not until I look back on photos that I see what's going on around us. This didn't just happen in New York, it happened always. That connection and bond between us was and will always be so powerful and strong.

Later that day when the darkness began to fall, we took a trip up to the top of the new One World Trade Centre where; not only did we feel it but we really were on top of the World.

Next day was a full-on day, first stop was Grand Central Train Terminal where we had lunch in the food court. I had seen this magnificent building in movies and always wanted to see it. Sharon always wanted to ice skate in Central Park, so this was our next destination. We walked around part of the park crossing over Bow Bridge where we stopped for a selfie whilst on our way to the open-air ice rink.

We spent around an hour on the ice, I had remembered that Sharon was pretty good at skating, compared to me. I ended up falling over at least three times whereas Sharon managed to keep her jeans dry.

In the evening, we had a meal in Times Square and afterwards went to the Top of the Rock viewing observatory, which is situated on top of the Rockefeller Centre.

Next day the theme for tall skyscrapers continued with a visit to the Empire State Building.

Out of all the skyscrapers that we visited; it was this one that we enjoyed the most. Stepping out onto the open viewing platform and feeling the wind in your face, really takes your breath away. The architecture of this building stands out from the others and is such an iconic building with its 1930's art deco design.

Prior to our trip to New York many people said to us about the shopping experiences and that we must go to the shopping malls. To be honest Sharon and I were never into shopping. If we ever had to get something, we would be in and out of the shops as quick as possible. We didn't want to spend our time in New York shopping for trainers or cheap designer clothes, this really wasn't us.

The following day we did however go to Macy's and the reason for this was to get a Christmas decoration for our tree.

That night we went to see the best Christmas show that we have ever seen. I had booked up about four weeks earlier for us to attend the opening night of the Radio City Hall, Christmas Spectacular with the Rockettes. This really got us into the Christmas spirit.

On our final day, we went for a walk across Brooklyn Bridge, and spent some time there before returning to Times Square, where we had a meal before making our way back to our hotel, where a private cab had been booked to take us back to the airport.

Summing up our trip to New York and the wedding proposal It was absolutely wonderful, fantastic and magical. New York will always be a special place to me and even though there were things that we didn't get to see, I would never go back there because I have those wonderful memories of our time there, the laughs we had, the places we visited and of course that special night when I got down on one knee and asked the love of my life to marry me.

Chapter Twenty-Seven
Living Together

We landed back in the UK on Sunday 15th November 2015 at around 08.00hrs, we collected my car from the off-site airport car park and made our way back home together. This was our first day of living together in our rented home in Writtle, near Chelmsford.

I hadn't lived with anybody for a number of years and you may think that I would be apprehensive; that wasn't the case, I was actually really excited about living together and I think that the timings worked out perfectly; we were a newly engaged couple starting out together.

We shared our home with Sharon's youngest son which was no problem at all, we hardly ever saw him as he would spend most of the time in his room watching sport on the TV.

For Sharon's birthday night, 17th November, just the two of us went out to a local restaurant. I think Sharon was disappointed that she didn't see any of her family, but what she didn't realise is that I had organised a surprise celebration. On the night of Friday, 20th November 2015, I took her out for a meal to a Chinese Buffet Restaurant, however I had arranged for Sharon's daughter and grandson, and her son to be there along with my children Jason, Mia and their partners. As I briefly mentioned earlier, there were issues between Sharon and her eldest son, so unfortunately, he and his family were not there to celebrate her birthday.

We entered the restaurant, which is quite large with lots of tables and seating. Over to our left was our table, Sharon at first didn't notice the family; it wasn't until we got closer that she spotted her grandson and everyone cheered, Sharon was so surprised. We had a lovely evening, and all sang happy birthday when a cake with candles was brought over to the table.

As Christmas 2015 approached we had great fun going out finding our first real tree, and on 11 December, we spent the afternoon decorating it, making sure that our Macy's tree decoration was in the line of sight from every chair in our lounge. Red and white fairy lights complemented the green pine needles. An angel wearing a gold-coloured silk dress, sat firmly at the top looking down on everyone. We loved our tree, and in the evening, we sat on the sofa with our feet up listening to Christmas songs while we ate cheese and biscuits. We spoke about what presents we were going to buy the family and made our Christmas plans.

In a conversation that we had during the summer months, Sharon told me that she always wanted a dressing table for her bedroom. Unfortunately, there was not enough room in the bedroom that she shared with her sister when she was younger. I remembered this conversation and planned to surprise Sharon with a dressing table as one of her Christmas Presents. On 22 December 2015, we were both on day shifts at work, so I arranged for the flat pack dressing table to be delivered. That night I was able to get off work early; I got home and there was the huge cardboard box in the entrance hall. I had about an hour and half to get it upstairs and built before Sharon got home, luckily, I finished it with ten minutes to spare. I placed a photo of us in a heart shaped frame and draped some red tinsel over it. Sharon got home and I asked her to come into the bedroom, she was so happy, she had tears in her eyes.

Sharon loved her dressing table and she would always sit at it whenever doing her hair or makeup. Today, even though I have moved home, I still have Sharon's dressing table in the bedroom with her perfumes and lotions on it just as she had them. I look in the mirror and think of all those times when my wife looked in it. I wish that I could see her reflection again.

On Christmas day 2015, we were both working, Sharon at the hospital and me at the fire station. So, we gave our presents to one another on Christmas Eve, 24th December. We had music playing and candles lit, the gas fire had been on for some time, making the coals glow a deep orange colour. I handed Sharon the ring box wrapped in gold paper. As she opened it, I said the following; "I know eternity rings are traditionally given for the birth of a new baby or a special anniversary, however, for me eternity means forever. So, I wanted to give you this ring which complements your engagement ring, and to show you that our love we have will last for all eternity." Sharon was overwhelmed and had tears in her eyes, as I slipped the ring onto her finger.

(In March 2020, my daughter, Mia, celebrated her twenty-first birthday and I wanted to give her something special. So, I gave her Sharon's eternity ring as an everlasting gift of love from the both of us.)

On Christmas day, my sister, Angela, invited Sharon and myself round for dinner. Sharon finished work before me and drove straight there after work, I came along when I finished my shift and got to Angela's around 20.30hrs. My sister and her family had dinner earlier, however, Sharon insisted that we ate our Christmas dinner together and waited for me to get there.

The next day, Boxing Day, 26th December we had Sharon's family and my family around for dinner and afterwards we played games. Sharon always got the latest game and in 2015, "Pie Face" was a best seller. We had so much fun with this.

Looking at this photo, you can see the Christmas cards on the shelf behind, these being our first fiancée/fiancé cards. Sharon and I kept every card that we sent to each other.

Every now and then I take them out of the box where they are kept, read the words and run my fingers over Sharon's hand writing. Yes, I feel sad and get tearful at times, but mostly I feel happiness when my thoughts take me back to the moments when Sharon handed me the cards.

Living together was just perfect in every way, even the simplest thing like food shopping together was fun; we generally would stop off for a coffee somewhere and just enjoy each other's company.

Chapter Twenty-Eight
Wales Road Trip

On 18 March 2016, we started our road trip of Wales, leaving home early we headed West and took the M4 motorway. Like previous road trips we were armed with our plug-in fridge, flask, camping stove and chairs. Once we crossed over the Severn Bridge into South Wales, we found a budget hotel where we stayed the night.

Next morning after breakfast, our journey continued towards the coast where we stopped at St David's Head. The weather was wet and cold, but that didn't stop us from walking around the bay and on to the rock formation known as St David's Head. Lunch consisted of hot soup and roll cooked on our stove and a cuppa from the flask.

We left the coast and made our way to our next bed and breakfast. (I cannot remember where it was, but I can remember that it was in a quaint little village). We passed some beautiful countryside, streams and rivers meandered through the valleys, the air was fresh and we were the only car on the road for miles.

We had such a laugh taking this photo; I had to put my phone on timer and propped it up using nearby rocks, however it kept falling over and after several shots of the sky, the rocks and even of my back side this was the final result.

We carried on and found a deserted picnic area where we stopped for a cuppa from our flask. I took the photo on the next page of Sharon sitting on a stone slab, she looked so beautiful. Whilst we were there, I had a strange thought, I remember thinking that if anything ever happened to Sharon I would come back to this place. I even took a photo of the sign; it was a place called Cwm Berwyn. I have no idea why I thought this; remember this was before any diagnosis.

To be honest it wasn't the first time that I had these thoughts. Maybe something or someone was trying to give me a subconscious sign. Maybe it was because I was so happy, yet I was also so scared of the thought of ever losing Sharon and I guess that this was another reason why I took so many photos, videos and selfies to capture those special moments.

The highlight of our road trip of Wales was in the north where we spent two nights in a hotel in Llanberis, at the bottom of Mount Snowdon.

Day one was spent driving around the local area and stopping off at pretty villages and we even visited a waterfall, which you would normally have to pay to view. However, the closed sign was up, yet the gate was unlocked, so we sneaked in and went down the flight of steps to a viewing platform. The water crashing down the rocks; sounding like thunder and the cold spray hitting our faces was invigorating. On the way out, there was a full height turnstile, the type you get at football stadiums and yes you guessed right, it was well and truly locked, so we had to climb over a fence to get to the gate we had used to get in. In Llanberis, there is a lake, where in the afternoon we went on a steam train ride around it, where the views of the mountain rising up are outstanding.

Next day we were going up Mount Snowdon. Ok, we didn't walk up; instead, we took the special mountain train which slowly rattles its way up. It couldn't take us up to the summit because the winter snow still covered the peak, and the train track disappeared under 3 feet of snow in places. We did manage to get quite a way up, and we could have carried on walking up to the top, but the train guide said that the weather conditions up there were bad, so we chose not to risk it. Instead, we stayed where the train had dropped us off and enjoyed the breath-taking scenery. We hadn't seen snow together before and we were like children stepping out onto the white covering and playing for the first time. Sharon pushed me over, I sank in the snow up to my knees and she pelted me with snowballs.

In case you were wondering, I rested my phone on a post and took a video of us mucking about, and then took screenshots from it.

After about an hour of playing in the snow, we began our descent along the rocky pathway. Walking down we were greeted with clear blue sky and bright sunshine. We took our time as we wanted to savour everything that we saw. Again, I set the phone up to take a selfie and this photo just shows how happy we were.

The final destination of our road trip was heading eastwards away from Snowdon, where we found a slate mine museum. We donned our safety helmets and climbed into a small cage which took us deep underground, where we were given an informative guide of how the Welsh slate used to be mined many years ago.

Our next stop was in a spa hotel on the Welsh Borders, where we stayed for one night before making our way back into England. On the way, we stopped off at Sharon's aunt and uncle's home, where they were kind enough to let us stay for the night.

Next day we began the four-hour journey home but of course we made a day of it and stopped off a couple of times.

Chapter Twenty-Nine
Isle of Wight

For my birthday, 28 April 2016, Sharon had booked up for a few days away in a Hotel on the Isle of Wight, which sits off the south coast of England. I didn't know anything about where we were going, all I was told by Sharon was that we were going away and to pack accordingly.

On 27 April, we set off in the car, I was driving and following the sat-nav directions, which Sharon had loaded in before I had got in the car. I found it really strange driving and having no idea where I was going, I was excited but also felt anxious. We were heading South along the motorway where we stopped at the services for a toilet break and a cuppa. Sharon didn't say anything about our destination, she kept it a secret.

It was when we got closer to Portsmouth and I could see road signs for the Isle of Wight Ferry, that Sharon told me where we were going and that the ferry had been booked. We had about an hour wait before we could board, this gave us time to grab another coffee, and another toilet break!

Once on board we looked through some travel guides about the island and Sharon told me about where we were staying. The hotel was run by Warner Leisure Hotels, and had lots of daytime activities available and evening entertainment. Our room overlooked the sea and gardens and we were being catered on a full board basis. After checking in, we went for a stroll along the sandy beach. At one point, Sharon laid on the sand and made a sand angel, like a snow angel except done in the sand instead. We also did a little dance and the photo below is one of Sharon's moves.

Next morning was my birthday, 28 April 2016, and whilst I was in the shower, Sharon decorated the room with birthday banners and balloons, and also sprinkled blue and silver happy birthday confetti on the dressing table and small round coffee table, which was placed next to the window. It was another surprise which I was really taken aback by. On the bed were two cards, I opened the largest one first, it was so lovely to read the words 'For My Special Fiancé'. The smaller card, Sharon had hand made. Remember the long stem red roses that I had asked to be placed on our table, on the evening cruise in New York, when I proposed? Well, Sharon brought a couple of the roses home with her and pressed them in a book, which I had no idea about. She made a birthday card and took the pressed petals, glued them in a heart shape, and sprinkled it with red sparkling glitter which caught the light from every direction.

I love all the cards that Sharon gave me and I have kept them all, but this handmade card has to be my favourite, I look at it and think of her making it, picking up the delicate petals one by one and sticking them down. The card is personal to me and I shall cherish it always.

After breakfast, we headed off on a trip around the island, first stopping at a local zoo. Sharon loved wildlife and was interested in animals. In the four years that I had with her, we visited many safari parks and zoos.

Our next stop was The Needles, this is a row of three stacks of chalk, rising thirty metres out of the sea just off the western side of the island. We had booked in advance a boat trip from the beach jetty to take us around The Needles. To get down to the beach we took a cable car, and the views of the different colours of rock are fantastic. The funny thing about our boat trip, was that a local primary school had also booked the same boat. There we were, sat amongst thirty excited eight- and nine-year-olds. For the duration of the trip, Sharon and I felt like we had gone back in time to our childhood, we even got involved with the questions the teachers were asking the children. I struggled with some of the answers and sometime found myself trying to sink down in the seat and hide so the teacher wouldn't pick me; however, being six feet four inches tall, it was quite difficult to lose myself.

Back on the beach, we sat for a while and looked at the sea, we laughed about our little school boat trip. It's when things like this happen, which make the memories so special and unique to Sharon and I.

We arrived back at the hotel in the late afternoon where we spent time relaxing before evening dinner. Little did I know that Sharon had told the restaurant that it was my birthday. Our table had been decorated with balloons and as we approached it, people on the other tables cheered and wished me happy birthday. The meal was really nice but the best part of the evening for me was that I was there with Sharon.

Chapter Thirty
Summer 2016

It was around May/June time that Sharon's mum had to go into hospital, following a fall that she had at home, and after spending some time in a hospital ward, she was transferred to a care home, which was within the hospital grounds. As Sharon worked in the same hospital, she would often call in to see her mum after her shifts had finished, and even popped over to the care home whilst she was on her lunch break.

There were many occasions that we both went to visit her and she was so pleased to see us. On warm days, we would take her into the gardens for some fresh air. On some days in the care home, a musician would come in and play for the residents. Sharon and I would sit at the back of the room and watch, it was a pleasure to see her mum join in and sing along. I used to enjoy going to see her mum and even though she was in a care home with other residents, I soon got used to the place and would always make a point of engaging in conversation with the other men and women. Most of them were similar to Sharon's mum and were suffering dementia. I remember one gentleman, who would sit all alone and he hardly spoke to anyone, that was until I started to talk about what he used to do as a job. He told me that he had worked for Ford Motor Plant in Dagenham, well that was it then, we both chatted away for ages, talking about different cars, which ones he preferred and what he used to do on the production line. After our first conversation, the nurses told me that he no longer sat alone and he would openly talk to people.

Whenever Sharon and I visited her mum, this gentleman would always acknowledge me and yes; we would have the same conversation over and over again, but you know something; I never got fed up with hearing about his past.

One day on our way home from seeing Sharon's mum, I said to Sharon how lovely it would be to be able to take her mum out for the day to Southend. So, this is exactly what we did, we spoke with the nurses and got permission and we borrowed a wheel chair. It was 18 August 2016; the weather was sunny and warm. We took blankets from home to keep her mum warm as she felt the cold.

I parked the car near to The Arches cafes, where we stopped and had fish and chips for lunch. Both Sharon and I were surprised by how much her mum ate, for a lady who usually didn't eat much, on this occasion she managed to clear the plate. After lunch, we walked in the direction of the pier, the tide was in and like I said previously, Southend looks so much nicer when you cannot see the mud. We stopped at Rossi Ice Cream parlour and sat on a bench opposite while we ate it. It was difficult to push the wheelchair and eat an ice cream at the same time. We went into the Adventure Island theme park, which was once known as Peter Pan's Playground, situated adjacent to the pier.

Sadly, the next day, her mum didn't remember much about the trip to Southend and I could see that Sharon was getting upset by this. I held Sharon's hand and said that her mum had a lovely time and that it was all about that moment which mattered, we both knew she enjoyed it and we had made another lovely memory for us. We hoped that we would be able to take her mum out again, unfortunately we were restricted by the weather as Autumn was soon to be upon us.

Looking back at the photos and videos I have of that day; I feel sad that the two beautiful ladies who were with me, are now no longer with us. But at the same time, I feel privileged to have been there; on what turned out to be the last time Sharon's mum went out on a day trip.

Summer of 2016 was a busy time for us, you have already read about the Rod Stewart and Lionel Ritchie concerts that we went to, as well as the Let's Rock Festival. Also, you have read about our holiday with my family to Devon in August.

It was at the end of June that we went to Cyprus for two weeks. Sharon had some money from the sale of her marital house and wanted to pay for her family and myself to all go away.

We stayed in a luxury 5-star hotel overlooking a natural horse show bay, which was ideal for snorkelling. It was really lovely being away with her family.

We spent ages on that inflatable Lilo, at times we all tried to climb on it and we spent most of the time underwater!

On one of the days, we went on a pirate boat trip, which was really great, dropping anchor in secluded bays, where we were able to swim and snorkel in the crystal-clear waters.

When we got home from holiday in Cyprus, we both spoke about another holiday for the two of us, so armed with the laptop we found a holiday in Cape Verde for November, in fact we would be away on Sharon's birthday.

Chapter Thirty-One
First Signs

At the time, I didn't think it was anything…

Remember I told you how Sharon struggled to go off to sleep straight away; well, it was towards the end of summer 2016 going into autumn that I noticed that Sharon was getting tired. We would cuddle up on the couch and more and more often she would drift off to sleep in my arms. It wasn't just at night, there were also times during the day where Sharon would say she felt exhausted. We didn't think much of it, we just put it down to shift work and over doing things. We just carried on as normal.

This is a very short chapter. But wanted you readers to be made aware of it now.

Chapter Thirty-Two
Wedding Plans

It was our second anniversary of meeting, 8 September 2016. We revisited the coffee shop in Stock where we first met, and then went on to Southend. Sitting on 'Sharon and Russell's' bench we spoke about lots of things, but the main topic of conversation was our wedding.

In 2017, we were both going to be fifty years old, and I always wanted to do something special. Sharon had never been on a cruise; it was something that didn't really appeal to her, and she was worried about getting sea sickness. I have been on a cruise of the Mediterranean before and really enjoyed it. I reassured Sharon that you can't feel the ship moving.

We spoke about maybe getting married on a cruise ship, the whole concept was that we would both be celebrating our fiftieths, getting married and having a honeymoon at the same time.

On the way home from Southend, we stopped off at a travel agent in Billericay High Street, and went in to discuss what we had been talking about. At precisely 17.22hrs, we left the shop where we had just booked our wedding day and cruise.

We were booked on a cruise of the Caribbean for two weeks, leaving the UK from Gatwick airport on 4th November 2017. Our wedding day was scheduled for 9th November, which was a day where we would be at sea.

We were so excited; all we spoke about on the way home, was about the wedding. What should we wear? Could we set up a video link so that our families could watch us on our special day? This was going to be the only downside of getting married on the cruise, our families and friends couldn't be there. We decided that we would have a reception party when we got back.

We were so excited about sharing our news, the first person Sharon wanted to tell was her daughter. That evening she came round to our house, and when Sharon told her the news; she cried and ran upstairs, Sharon followed her.

She was happy for us, but sad that we would be on our own, on a ship with no family there. Sharon explained that it was what we both chose and that the reception back here in the UK would be where we could all celebrate with family and friends.

If my memory serves me correct, I believe I phoned Jason and Mia that evening and told them our happy news. It was on 11 September 2016 that Sharon and I went to a music festival in Hyde Park London, with my sister Angela and her husband Daniel. Whilst we were on the train travelling to London, we told them the news of our wedding plans, and they were very happy for us. Sharon and Angela had a good relationship with each other and they became very close.

We went to see my mum and dad the next day and told them about our wedding plans. They were obviously very happy for us, but I could see and sense that my dad was sad, he wanted to be part of our special day. We did play it down a bit, by saying although we were getting married on the cruise, the main celebrations would be at the reception in this country. We would still have a top table and do speeches and other traditional things.

So, the cruise and wedding were booked, next we had to find a venue where we could have a wedding reception. After searching the internet and ringing around various halls, Sharon was told about The Reid Rooms, a wedding venue in Margaret Roding, a rural village about fifteen minutes from where we lived, so we arranged a viewing for 11 October 2016.

The venue was ideal for what we wanted, we explained that we were getting married on the cruise and that we wanted a reception party to celebrate with our families and friends. That day we made a booking for the venue.

Sharon told me that it was her dad's birthday at the end of the month, so I suggested that we could take him out for a meal and at the same time tell him about the wedding. In a conversation that Sharon and I had some time ago, I remembered her saying that her dad liked the singer Petula Clark. So, I searched the internet to see if she still done live shows, and it turned out that she would be performing at the Cliffs Pavilion in Southend. I rang and managed to get three tickets and book a pre-show meal for 15 October 2016.

We all had a lovely night and it was such a pleasure to see Sharon's dad enjoy the show. We did tell him at the preshow meal about the wedding and he was so happy for us. Sharon chose not to say anything to her mum because she didn't want to cause any confusion. Remember, her mum was in a care home suffering with dementia. We would see how well she was nearer the time.

Chapter Thirty-Three
The Diagnosis

On 16 October 2016, I was on day shift at the fire station, and got home around 20.45hrs. Sharon was watching Coronation Street on TV. I made us both a drink and then Sharon switched off the TV and we spoke about our day. This was something we always did, the tele would go off and we would talk and listen to music. Occasionally we would watch something together but certainly after we had been to work, we would make sure we had no distraction from the tele; it was now our time.

We went up to bed about 23.00hrs and were passionate with each other, and it was whilst we were making love that I felt a small pea size lump in Sharon's left breast. I didn't say anything straight away as I didn't want to spoil the moment. Afterwards, when we were relaxing, I asked Sharon if she ever checked her breasts for any lumps or bumps. She replied, no she never did. I never told Sharon that I found the lump, I just suggested that she should check herself. Whilst laying down next to me, she lifted her left arm and with her right hand examined her left breast. She went straight to the lump that I had found. By now, we were both sitting on the edge of the bed, she felt her right breast and couldn't find anything. Sharon then asked me to check for her, and I said yes there is definitely something there. Sharon seemed fairly relaxed about it and said that she would get it checked at the doctors.

Next day at the doctors, Sharon was examined by her GP. The Doctor said to her it is nothing to worry about, probably just a blocked duct or small cyst, however, to put minds at rest a mammogram was requested. So that was it, the appointment for the mammogram came through for 24 October 2016. The week-long wait, from the 16th to the 24th was normal, we had nothing to be concerned about as the doctor wasn't concerned. The mammogram was just a formality.

The 24th came, I was working on day shift and Sharon was also on day shift at the hospital. The day before, I had asked her if she wanted me to be there, and she said that there is no need as it will all be fine. Sharon had told her colleagues that she had an appointment and had to book off duty for an hour. The plan was for her to go straight back to her ward afterwards.

It was early afternoon whilst I was at work that my phone rang, fortunately I wasn't on a call, and was at the fire station. It was Sharon, she was crying, her words were muddled and I could hardly understand what she was saying. I reassured her and asked her to take deep breaths and tell me again.

The radiographer who had done the mammogram was certain it was breast cancer. Sharon was still in the breast unit and was crying. She couldn't go back to work and needed to go home. I did the same, I told my guvnor that I had to leave straight away to be with Sharon.

That forty-five-minute journey seemed to take forever, I felt numb, I was crying and I was scared. When I got home, I held Sharon in my arms and hugged her, we cried and I mean we really cried lots. Sharon wanted to talk to her daughter and rang her to ask her to come round. When she arrived, I took her son out into the garden so Sharon could talk to her daughter alone. I didn't want for him to see or hear his mum and nan getting upset. Sharon's youngest son, who was living with us, came home from work and was given the sad news.

A few weeks before all of this, I had encouraged and suggested that perhaps Sharon and her eldest son could go out for a meal and try and sort things out. Thankfully, whatever differences there had been, were put behind them that night.

It must have been around 20.30hrs when I took Sharon to see her eldest son, so that she could tell him of the mammogram.

Later that night when it was just the two of us at home, we cried again as we tried to understand it. Sharon had already been assigned a breast care nurse, and had been given some leaflets containing information about breast cancer, and what to expect.

A week passed and Sharon had to go for a biopsy of the lump. A few more days to wait and we had an appointment with an oncologist to get the results. It was confirmed to us that it was cancer, triple negative breast cancer, to be precise. We were told that this is the worse type of breast cancer. Fortunately, because we had caught it early and because Sharon was otherwise fit and healthy, everything was looking positive.

An appointment was made for Sharon to have a lumpectomy, a procedure where the lump and surrounding tissue is surgically removed whilst under general anaesthetic. The date of the operation was to be on 30 November 2016.

We asked if it would still be ok to travel, as we had a holiday booked in Cape Verde. The oncologist said yes, it's important that we both go away as planned and have a nice time.

So, that's what we did…

Chapter Thirty-Four
Cape Verde

Our holiday to Cape Verde began on 14 November 2016.

One thing I will say, is that we didn't talk about, or mention the cancer at all for the whole duration of the holiday; except for one time. That was when we were on the beach sunbathing, and about to go in the sea for a swim. Sharon looked at me and said, "I am going to go topless, as it may be the last time, I will be able to." She removed her bikini top and sunbathed for a while before going into the sea. That was the only time it was mentioned, however, even though we had a lovely holiday, I knew what was going through my mind and I am pretty sure Sharon's thoughts were all over the place as well.

So, let me tell you about our holiday.

When we originally booked it, we wanted somewhere relatively quiet and warm and Sal Island was just what we expected. Beautiful golden sandy beaches gently sloping into a clear blue sea. Our hotel was made up of apartments within a big complex, we were all inclusive and there was a large selection of foods from all over the world with speciality restaurants dotted here and there within the grounds.

In the evenings after dinner, we would go for a walk along the beaches and watch the stunning sunsets, this was normally followed by drinks back at the hotel and dancing to the live entertainment.

Cape Verde is so relaxed and the locals are just as relaxed; there are signs which read 'No Stress', and this is exactly what we needed.

The seed had been planted; the woman I loved to bits has breast cancer; my head was full of emotions and questions. Was it going to be cured, how would we cope, why has she got it, did we catch it early, would she have to have a mastectomy, and that nagging question in my head was, would she die? I had no answers to these questions except the how would we cope? I would do my upmost best for my beautiful fiancée; I would help her and support her and take care of her always.

Whilst we were on our holiday, it was Sharon's birthday, 17 November 2016, and on that day, we decided to do a jeep excursion of the island. But first I had to give Sharon her birthday present. It was forty-seven minutes past midnight when I handed Sharon a present. I wanted her to have it then, as in the morning we had to be up early for breakfast and our trip. She tore the gift wrapping off, revealing a travel guide of Rome.

Before Sharon was diagnosed, I had booked up for us to go to Rome. Our holiday in Cape Verde was to finish on 21 November, and we were due to fly out to Rome on the next day. So, you could imagine I was a little nervous, what if there were any flight delays.

On the morning of Sharon's birthday, we were up and out early for breakfast. Our meeting point for the excursion was on the beach, and the time we had to be there was 09.00hrs.

Four jeeps were in a line; we made ourselves known and were allocated the blue jeep. We had the option to sit inside or on the back which was in the open. Our driver did warn us that it would be dusty. We chose the back, there were two other couples on our jeep. But being as we were first there, we got the best seats, right up next to the bulkhead. Here we were able to stand up and hold on and feel the wind and dust in our faces.

The excursion included stopping off at many places of interest around the island. We even had time to visit a salt-lake, where you can go in the water and relax, I say relax because it is so difficult to swim; due to the density of the water which is enriched with minerals, you just float on the surface. Our guide told us that the lake had good healing powers and would keep us young and healthy; if only this was true!

We had a brilliant day but most of all Sharon's birthday was full of making special memories. A photographer took many photos of the day. I love to look back at these and to see the joy on Sharon's face makes me feel like it was just yesterday.

Next day we spent the morning by the pool, it was huge and even had a swim-up bar, which we both took advantage of; Sharon had strawberry daiquiri cocktails and I had the non-alcoholic pina colada.

Whilst sitting at the bar we were handed a pencil and paper and took part in the quiz; I was glad that Sharon was on my side because she got every question correct.

After lunch, we made our way to the beach and relaxed on the sun loungers, Sharon was looking at the Rome travel guide, and we were talking and planning the things we wanted to see.

After a while, Sharon got up and walked down to the sea, I felt that she wanted to be on her own for a little while. As I watched her looking out to sea, I had tears in my eyes, she looked so perfect, her blonde hair catching the sunlight and she looked so well; yet there was this nasty thing growing inside her. I quickly dried my eyes before Sharon turned and walked back. Nothing at all was said yet we both sensed that we had been having an emotional moment.

As I look at this photo, I wonder what Sharon was really thinking about at the time. I do hope that she was having nice thoughts as she looked out over the bright blue sea.

Chapter Thirty-Five
Romantic Rome

We arrived home from Cape Verde on 21 November 2016 around 23.00hrs, and our flight to Rome was on the next day at about 08.00hrs. As soon as we got in, we unpacked and washed clothes and repacked. We did go to bed but it was only for a few hours because we had to be up early to travel to the airport. As tiring as it was, it was still exciting; we had never done anything like this before.

We checked into the hotel in Rome in the afternoon. When I originally booked it, I spent ages researching where to stay. I wanted to be close to the main attractions but at the same time in a nice area. I finally chose the Hotel Relais 95 Trevi, which is about fifty meters from Trevi Fountain. Our room was on the third floor but unfortunately the lifts were faulty, so we had to take the stairs. The room was tastefully decorated, and I remember that the ceiling was very high and had been painted with a special paint. At night, once the lights were turned out, thousands of tiny stars began to twinkle; just like a real night sky. At the end of our days, we would lay there talking and watching the 'stars', we had our own planetarium.

After unpacking and logging into the free Wi-Fi, we went for a walk. I knew that we were close to Trevi Fountain but didn't realise how close. We left the hotel and turned right passing souvenir shops and some Italian designer clothes stores. There were many tourists but it wasn't over crowded; I had read many reviews which stated that Rome is packed with tourists, however, during the whole time that we were there it was relatively quiet, and even the locals that we spoke to, said that it was normally much busier. We were glad because we were able to take our time and get to see the attractions.

As we approached the fountain, I was watching Sharon, to see what her reaction would be as Trevi Fountain came into view. Her mouth was open and she was shocked by the sheer beauty and size of this wonderful piece of architecture. Whilst we were on the beach in Cape Verde, just a couple of days before, we had read in our travel guide about the myth of throwing coins into the fountain, originating from the 1954 movie, *'Three Coins in the Fountain'*, and it goes like this;

If you throw one coin, *you will return to Rome.*
If you throw two coins, *you will fall in love with an attractive Italian.*
If you throw three coins, *you will marry the person that you met.*

We stood back and watched to see what others were doing, it seemed like the thing to do was to stand with your back towards the fountain, and then throw your coins over your shoulder. We were already planning our wedding and we weren't planning on falling in love with an Italian, so that just left us to throw one coin each; that we would return to Rome and we also made our own individual wishes. Sharon went first and threw her coin in, I asked if she had made a wish, she replied, "I've made my wish." My turn next to throw my coin and to make that wish. Now I can only assume that Sharon's wish was the same as mine, but I will never know for certain. My wish was; for Sharon to make a full recovery from the cancer and that we would live happily ever after.

Sadly, my wish didn't come true!

We stopped again at the fountain later that night, where the ambience was so much different from earlier; hardly anyone was there, strategically placed lighting reflecting on the sculptured figurines, makes them look real. We both said that it was beautiful in daylight but so much more romantic at night time.

That night we had traditional Italian Pizza in the square opposite The Pantheon and watched the street performers.

The Pantheon is a former Roman Temple which is now a Catholic Church. From the outside, there is a shallow domed roof and a I consisting of many large granite columns, an outstanding piece of engineering and architecture, and considering that it was built between 113–125 AD it is in great condition. It's not until you step inside that the beauty of the marble and granite really takes your breath away. There are various areas where people were praying and lots of statues of Christ and other figures. Please excuse my ignorance; I mentioned earlier that I was not a religious person and my knowledge of the Catholic faith is very limited. With that said, whilst we were in Rome, every church and chapel that we went in we would both sit down and pray. We prayed for Sharon's cancer to go away, we prayed and prayed over and over again. This was totally out of my comfort zone, but I thought, *It's worth a go; let's see if there really is some almighty power that can help.*

Sadly, just like our wishes at the fountain, our prayers were never answered!

When I booked the Rome trip, I also booked excursions for us to have a guided tour of the Colosseum and The Roman Forum, as well as The Vatican and St Peters Basilica.

It's now our second day and we have a full day ahead of us. We didn't bother with taxis as we had read that traffic in Rome is rather busy, to be honest I am glad we chose to walk everywhere because we got to see more of this ancient city. We were off to visit the Colosseum, our guide was meeting us outside at 09.15hrs, and as you guessed we were there early, forty-five minutes early to be precise. This gave us time to grab a coffee from a nearby cafe and to have a quick walk around the outside of the oval shaped amphitheatre. The Colosseum is somewhere that I had always wanted to visit, this stems back to my martial arts days and my interest in Bruce Lee films. In a scene from *'The Way of The Dragon'*, Bruce has a fight with the American actor, Chuck Norris, within the arches of the Colosseum. I told Sharon about this and she had no idea what I was rambling on about.

Our guide took us in through a side door; I had paid extra when I booked it to avoid any potential crowds. We were both amazed by the knowledge of our guide and of the history that we learnt, for example the Colosseum used to be covered in marble, which was later removed and used in some of the construction of churches and chapels in Rome. The tour included access to the lower level, where the gladiators would have been held before going up a ramp or wooden lift to the arena above. We also went up to the higher levels and had breath-taking views. The next part of the tour was the Roman Forum where there are several ancient ruins of government buildings. We spent some time here and we sat for a while and we spoke about what it must have been like back in the day.

The weather in Rome was really mild for the time of year, we had packed coats and warm clothes but didn't need them. Armed with our city guide of Rome and map, we made our way to the Spanish Steps, which featured in the 1953 movie *'Roman Holiday'* starring Audrey Hepburn. I have never seen the film and I'm not certain if Sharon had, but somehow, she seemed to know the exact places to stand for a photo opportunity.

After a busy day, we made our way back to our hotel but first we stopped off and had dinner. We managed to find a restaurant that was reasonably priced and the atmosphere was really good, with seating being outside we were able to people watch; something Sharon and I did a lot of; we would try and find famous lookalikes amongst the people strolling past.

We finally got back to our hotel around midnight and we were both shattered.

Next morning, we were up early again for a continental breakfast on the roof top terrace of our hotel. Our day was planned out, a tour of Vatican City and the impressive St Peters Basilica.

Whilst in the Vatican we visited The Sistine Chapel; There were many signs which read NO PHOTOGRAPHY, and guards were positioned around the perimeter to enforce the rule. Well, my phone just happened to be in my hand and strangely enough the video record function must have turned on by itself! Later that night when we looked back over the day's photos, we came across some beautiful videos of Michelangelo's masterpiece that he had painted on the ceiling.

As we continued to walk around, we did wonder if we would see the Pope, which was highly unlikely, all the same we both said if he did make an appearance, we would ask him to use all his powers of prayer to take the cancer away. I have already mentioned that we were not religious, however we were willing to try anything to get rid of it.

After watching the changing of the guards outside in St Peters Square, we had a look around a souvenir shop and I came up with the idea; to each buy a post card and write on it, then send it to each other from the Vatican City post box. Our cards were delivered home about a week later, and it was so lovely to read what Sharon had written. I have not seen these cards for some time, I can only assume that Sharon put them in her memory box.

We returned home on 24 November 2016, and on the next day I had booked up a late birthday meal in a local restaurant for both Sharon's family and my family. It was a lovely evening.

Chapter Thirty-Six
Changes

Whilst in Rome, we spoke about our wedding plans, and were both in agreement that we now wanted to get married at home in the UK. We wanted to have our family and friends with us on our special day. The cruise was still going to happen as it would be Sharon's 50th birthday at the time, the only difference was we would not be getting married on the ship. I phoned the cruise company to explain our situation and they were very helpful and understanding.

We went back to the Reid Rooms and booked the wedding venue for 5 January 2018. I will talk more about our day later on in the book.

When thinking of a title for this chapter, it had to be 'changes', our lives changed from that very first diagnosis. We had been given an appointment book from the breast unit at the hospital, along with lots of leaflets with information about breast cancer. In my writing, you will notice that I use the word 'we', I am fully aware that it was Sharon who had the cancer, and who had to go through the harsh treatment plan. However, Sharon once said to me, "This does very much involve you, and I am very aware that your life has changed too". My reply to this was "We are in this together, I will stand by you, I will support you and always be there for you, but most of all I will love you for all eternity."

The date of the operation was 30 November 2016, but prior to this we had to attend the hospital for a preop assessment a few days before. The hospital where Sharon was to have the operation and later chemotherapy, is the same hospital where Sharon worked. As you can imagine the NHS employs a lot of staff on different shift rotas, but whenever we went for an appointment, Sharon always saw someone that she knew. Broomfield Hospital was to become my second home, I soon learnt all the short cuts to and from various departments and the best places to park the car. Parking for chemotherapy patients is free and they have their own parking area, however all the other times we had to go there, we had to pay. Sharon was against having to pay because she had already paid a large sum of money for her staff parking permit, so we used it whenever we had to attend the numerous appointments. Strangely to this day that permit, even though out of date, still sits tucked in the sun visor of my car. Another thing that I can't ever part with.

The morning of the 30th came and we had to be in the day surgery ward for 07.00hrs. We were shown to a side room where there was a bed and an armchair. A nurse checked Sharon's details and did some observations, it was quite funny because Sharon knew everything about taking patient observations, blood pressure, temperature, pulse and O2 levels and knew how to use the equipment. We sat in our assigned room until it was time for Sharon to be taken to the operating theatre.

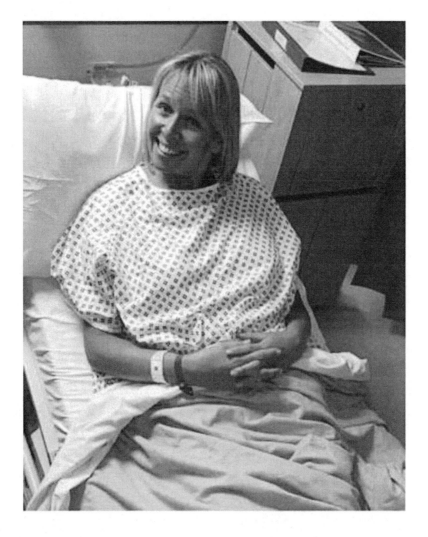

Just moments before an operation Sharon still managed to smile. Such a brave woman.

The porters came and took Sharon down to theatre, a nurse said that I should go and have lunch and to come back in around two hours. All of a sudden, I felt alone and lost, ok, I knew that she was in good hands and the doctor doing the surgery was highly experienced, all the same Sharon was being put to sleep, I couldn't be there to help if anything went wrong; but what could I possibly do anyway?

I went and sat in the coffee shop in the atrium of the hospital and phoned Sharon's children to say she had gone to theatre. It's the same coffee shop where I used to meet Sharon on her lunch break, I sat in the same seats. All manner of things were going through my mind; what would I do if she didn't come through? What if it was worse than the scans had shown? What if it was all a mistake and they found no tumour? How great that would have been. Sharon would be here now and I would not be writing this book.

After an hour and three coffees later, I went back to our side room to wait, I had to because I felt closer to Sharon there. I sat on the blue fake leather armchair and looked at the empty place where Sharon's bed was. Around an hour and half later Sharon was brought back to the room, a nurse said that the surgery had gone well and that the surgeon would be along shortly to have a chat. Sharon was able to get dressed in her own clothes, the nurse gave her a cup of tea and a chicken sandwich. The female surgeon told us that she had removed the tumour and surrounding tissue, and was confident that she had got everything, also as a precaution, she had removed some lymph nodes from under the arm, so these could be checked in the laboratory for abnormal cells.

A follow up appointment was made for two weeks' later. We were also given more leaflets with advice on things to do after an operation, as well as a course of antibiotics for Sharon. We were then finally allowed to go home.

Next day Sharon was able to remove the dressing on her breast, the surgeon had done an amazing job; she had used glue to stick the cut together, instead of stitches. This meant that there would be just a fine scar and due to the position of the incision, it was hardly noticeable when it fully healed. I did feel sad for Sharon, her breast was heavily bruised which continued up under her arm. In the afternoon, we both wanted to get some fresh air, so we went for a drive to Papermill Lock, a beautiful place on the Navigation Canal which runs from Heybridge Basin to Chelmsford.

I first went to Papermill Lock with my children when they were younger, and we would often go there for tea and cake from the tea room, before walking along the canal, looking at the narrow boats which are moored up. It wasn't long after I met Sharon that I mentioned about the lock and tea room, Sharon said that she had never been there before. So, this soon became a place where we would frequently visit. Nowadays, I often go there and sit alone in the same seat next to the lock gates, I have a tea and a slice of carrot cake and I lose myself in my thoughts of Sharon. I even take my note book and write chapters for this book.

Taken on 18 January 2017.

Our last time together at Papermill Lock, taken on 7 August 2018. Sharon's health had deteriorated a lot at this stage. Walking was difficult but she still wanted to do the normal things that we had always done.

At the follow up appointment, two weeks after the lumpectomy, we met with the surgeon and breast care nurse. We were told that the lymph nodes which were removed showed no cancerous cells, we both breathed a sigh of relief. Also, the surgeon confirmed again that she had removed the tumour and the surrounding tissues, so from what could be seen in the scans and from the operation; the cancer had been removed.

However, she said that being that it was triple negative breast cancer, the worst type, she wanted Sharon to have chemotherapy and radiotherapy. We mentioned to the surgeon that we had a cruise booked for November 2017 to celebrate Sharon's 50th birthday, we asked if we needed to cancel it. She replied, "No don't cancel it, you two go away and have an amazing holiday which you will both need."

The next time we were at the breast care unit was to meet the oncologist, where we were given a treatment plan and more information leaflets. The nurse explained that Sharon would lose her hair due to the chemo. I remember the sadness in Sharon's eyes as she said, "I wanted to have long hair for my wedding day." I put my arm around her and said, "You will look beautiful; you always look stunning." I don't think my words really helped, but I didn't know what else to say or do at that time, I just wanted to reassure her.

Chapter Thirty-Seven
Treatment Plan

Chemotherapy began on Friday 13 January 2017 and was scheduled for three Fridays out of four, every month and would last until the end of April.

The chemo suite is in the same hospital where Sharon worked, Broomfield Hospital in Chelmsford. The suite consists of a waiting room and within that room is a TV fixed to the wall, beneath that are rows and rows of leaflets relating to cancer and treatment. Adjacent to the waiting room there is a kitchen which we were able to use, and have complimentary tea, coffee and juice drinks, as well as a selection of sandwiches and biscuits. A corridor leads to a ward with two bays, consisting of blue vinyl reclining chairs and an upright chair next to it, these chairs are on three of the walls in each bay. I wonder why blue is used for the colour theme on hospital chairs? Small occasional tables separate each set of chairs.

Part of the process of chemo involved Sharon having a blood test every two weeks before the treatment to see if her white blood cells were not too low. So, this was another trip to the hospital, every second Wednesday afternoon, so that the results were available for the Friday.

Before we could go into the ward, we would be seen by a doctor who would check the blood results and ask questions on how Sharon had been feeling. The doctor would prescribe the various medications that Sharon needed whilst on the chemotherapy.

Once in the ward we were shown to a seat, Sharon had the recliner and I would sit next to her in an upright chair. It took between three and four hours, sometimes longer for each chemo session. For three sessions, Sharon was cannulated in the arm with a needle, and had to place her arm in a bucket of hot water, to raise her veins. It was becoming more difficult for the chemo nurses to find a vein. Sharon had developed cording, which is an irritation of the veins caused by the chemo, which in Sharon's case looked and felt like a web of thick, rope like structures/indentations under the skin. It affected her lower arm and elbow and caused her pain and tightness, to the point where she could not fully stretch her arm out. Sharon had to have many sessions of physiotherapy and a special cream was prescribed which she had to apply regularly. It took a few months for her arm to fully recover.

Because of this cording, Sharon was given a PICC line (Peripherally Inserted Central Catheter). This is a thin tube that is put in the upper arm. The line runs up and inside the vein in the arm and into the large vein in the chest just above the heart. The line is sealed with a special cap or bung, which is then attached to the drip or syringe containing the chemo or other medication. The drugs then flow freely, direct to the heart. When not in use, the special cap coming out of the arm is taped down and protected with a tubular bandage. Sharon was given a waterproof sleeve so she was able to shower. The PICC line stayed in place until chemotherapy finished at the end of April 2017.

Sharon used to fall asleep whilst having chemo, as for me I waited until she dozed off, then I would walk to the pharmacy in the atrium area to collect her medication. I would then come back and sit with her. I was allowed to use the small kitchen area to make tea for us and also the odd biscuit or two. We took a bag with word searches and magazines to help pass the time.

On one of the many visits to hospital, I asked if the tiredness Sharon had in the summer of 2016, could have been an early sign of cancer, and the consultant said it was very likely as the body reacts in different ways.

The first chemo session Friday 13 January 2017

With chemotherapy comes harsh side effects which vary depending on the type of chemo being used. Every cancer patient is different and has their own treatment plan.

Probably the most common and the most visual side effect is the loss of hair. I shall talk about this in a while but first let me tell you about the other side effects that Sharon suffered with:

Sickness; even though Sharon was on anti-sickness drugs she often felt sick and at times was sick.

Mouth sores; Chemo can cause mouth thrush and sores which Sharon had. She was prescribed medicated mouthwash and given drugs for the thrush.

Skin and nail changes; Sharon's nails became weak and brittle and her skin became dry in places. She would use a moisturiser to help control this.

Indigestion; Sharon suffered with this at times, but it was controlled with medication.

This brings me to hair loss; the leaflets and the nurses said the hair would start to fall out around ten to fourteen days after the first chemo. On 27 January 2017, we went out for an afternoon tea, by now Sharon's hair was beginning to fall out and become thin and patchy. She still managed to gently brush it. The next photo was taken on that day and this is the last photo I have of Sharon with her long blonde hair.

The following day I was at work, and I spoke to Sharon in the afternoon, she was really down and upset with her hair. When I got home, she was sitting in tears, she had her hair up in a band, I put my arms around her and we hugged. I reassured her that she will be fine and said it will grow back once chemo finishes. I asked if she wanted me to use my clippers and shave the remaining hair from her head. After a while, she said that it would probably be for the best to do it now. We went upstairs and Sharon sat on her dressing table stool while I started to shave her head. This was one of the hardest things I have done, however I held back my tears and emotions that night, I had to stay strong and focussed. I felt so sorry for Sharon she cried lots that night. She hated having to lose her hair.

I loved Sharon with hair or with no hair, as a matter of fact she had a lovely shaped head. She loved laying on my lap while I gently ran the tips of my fingers over the soft smooth skin on her head.

Next day she wore her wig for the first time, and she looked beautiful. Sharon only tended to wear it if we were going out for the evening, because it irritated her head and gave her a head ache. She had bought a lovely selection of chemo hats and scarfs which she always looked amazing in. The thing with chemo is that you not only lose your hair on your head; you lose it from everywhere, eyebrows and eye lashes included. With Sharon, it took longer for these to fall out. Hence in the photo on the next page you can still see her eye lashes. This photo was taken the day after I shaved her hair, and it is a wig that Sharon is wearing. Now, I am no hair or wig expert but I would say that it looks natural and almost like Sharon's own hair.

Even though we had a treatment plan and a routine, we both tried to do the 'normal' things we used to do, we still went out for afternoon teas, we still went out for walks and even managed to go away for a few days here and there. We had to be aware of our timings if we were travelling on public transport or mixing in a public environment, because chemotherapy also weakens the immune system by killing the white blood cells, which meant that Sharon could have contracted anything.

One side effect that I have not mentioned is fatigue. There were times when Sharon was physically and mentally exhausted. People tend to think of fatigue and tiredness as the same thing. Well, I have been tired and thankfully I have never been fatigued. They are two entirely different things. There was a time that Sharon and I went out midway through her chemo treatment, we decided to take a drive to Southend, remember like we used to do. I parked the car and we began to walk slowly in the direction of Rossi's ice cream parlour. Sharon managed about twenty-five meters and had to stop and sit down. She tried again after a fifteen-minute rest, but was struggling, she just couldn't find any energy to take even a few steps, so I helped her back to the car. Instead, I drove the car along the length of the sea front and parked up at Thorpe Bay overlooking the sea, I went across the road, bought two take away coffees and we sat in the car watching the boats bobbing around on the incoming tide.

One thing for certain during the treatment, we still carried on doing the things we loved.

Sharon's 'last' chemotherapy session was on 28 April 2017. For those who can remember back in the early chapters, this is my birthday and 2017 happened to be my fiftieth.

I spent my birthday in the chemo suite in the morning, Sharon happened to mention to the nurses that it was my fiftieth and halfway through the session they carried in two little cupcakes for me.

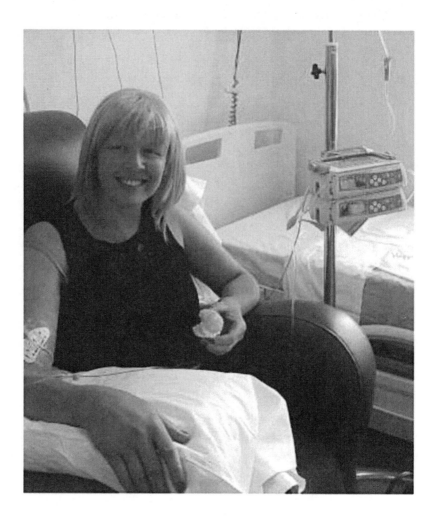

For me, the best birthday present was watching those last drops of red coloured drugs running down the tube and disappearing into Sharon's arm for the last time, and seeing the look of relief on her face when the PICC line was removed by a specialist nurse afterwards.

Once we had finished at the chemo suite, we walked over to the care home where Sharon's mum was. Sadly, her mum had deteriorated a few days before and was now at the end of her life. We spent the afternoon with her mum, holding her hand and comforting her; two days later on 30 April 2017, Sharon's mum passed away peacefully.

Sharon knew that on my birthday we would be in the chemo suite, so she secretly, with the help of my sister Angela, arranged a surprise birthday party at

Angela's house. This was on Saturday 22 April 2017, I had no idea and it was a total surprise.

We were off out to see Angela's new home for the first time. We were met by my sister at her front door and she started to show us around, as I opened a door which led into a large kitchen/dining area everyone shouted, "Surprise, Happy Birthday." There were balloons, banners and a table full of food. Sharon's family and my family were all there. It was such a wonderful party, and for Sharon to organise it whilst she was having treatment and with the upset of her mum being poorly; was such a special thing to do for me.

On the morning of my birthday when we had just woken up, Sharon handed me my card and another envelope, in it was details of a trip to Paris which Sharon had booked for us and was scheduled for the coming July. I will tell you more about the trip a bit later.

The treatment plan wasn't just chemotherapy; it also involved radiotherapy which commenced at the beginning of June 2017 and finished on 4 July 2017. Five days a week, Monday through to Friday, for a month we would travel to Colchester Hospital where Sharon had targeted radiotherapy to her left breast. We would get to the hospital early as Sharon's session was normally one of the first around 08.00hrs. This worked out well because the actual time we were in there was around an hour so that gave us the rest of the day to do other things. There were a couple of occasions when Sharon's daughter was able to take her, which allowed me to work.

Radiotherapy also had its own side effects; with Sharon these were a slight skin reaction in the area being treated as well as tiredness and fatigue. There are many other side effects but thankfully, she didn't suffer from those.

The last day of radiotherapy was 4 July 2017. We were so happy that all treatment had now finished; no more hospital appointments, just a yearly mammogram on the anniversary of the diagnosis. Once the session had finished, we drove straight to Bournemouth and Sandbanks, which is near Poole in Dorset for a few days' rest and recuperation.

Last day at the radiotherapy centre, 4 July 2017

Chapter Thirty-Eight
Getting Stronger

We spent one night in Bournemouth followed by two nights in Sandbanks. We couldn't have asked for better weather; it was hot and sunny and we were able to spend the days on the beautiful sandy beaches, we even went swimming in the sea, well not quite swimming more like floating and bouncing around on the waves. This break was just what we both needed. Sharon was fatigued and even found it hard work walking in the soft sand. One evening we bought a disposable BBQ, which we set up on the beach and cooked steak, which we had with a healthy salad. It was whilst we were there, watching the sun set, that Sharon said she needed to get fit again. She had put weight on whilst she had been on the treatment because she had not been as active as she was before the diagnosis. I also needed to lose weight and get fit again. So, we both agreed to support each other and eat healthily and start to exercise.

It took a month for the side-effects from the radiotherapy to ease off and for the fatigue to go. We were eating healthy foods and going out for walks, each time our walks would get longer and we would get quicker. Sharon was given access to a gym and started to go there. I used the gym at the fire station and together, our efforts soon began to show. We both felt so much better in ourselves and we enjoyed the shopping for and the cooking of healthy recipes. In just four months, Sharon had lost 1.5 stone (21 pounds) or (9.252 in kg) in weight and I had lost 4.5 stone (63 pounds) or (28.576 in kg).

Chapter Thirty-Nine
Bonjour Paris

My birthday present that Sharon gave me was a trip to Paris. It was early morning on 28 July 2017 that we made our way to Ebbsfleet International train station in Kent. By mid-morning, we had arrived at Paris Nord train station. A taxi took us to our hotel which was a five-minute walk from the Eiffel Tower. We checked in, showered and changed clothes before heading out. Sharon had prebooked tickets for a boat trip on The Seine later that afternoon, and then for us to visit the top of the Eiffel Tower in the evening.

Sharon had given me on my birthday back in April, an engraved brass padlock with two keys. The idea was to bring it to Paris and lock it to a bridge. We walked around and found the Flame of Liberty, a full-size gold-leafed replica of the Statue of Liberty flame in New York. Which happens to be near to the tunnel where Princess Diana tragically lost her life. The statue has evolved into a memorial for the Princess. Candles, flowers, private letters and newspaper cuttings are placed around the bottom of the statue. A chain link fence about two feet from the ground surrounds the flame and it was here where we chose to attach the padlock, amongst the many others already there. I wonder if the lock is still in place, I would like to think so. Engraved on the lock is: Sharon & Russ 8/9/2014 xxxxxx. This being the date when we first met.

We made our way back to The Seine where we boarded the river cruise boat and went up to the top deck, where we found the perfect seats, right at the front. As we sailed down the river, we had uninterrupted views of the Louvre and of Notre Dame Cathedral.

Following on from this we had a coach tour around the city which was really nice as it was dusk and the tower was lit up with flashing lights. The driver stopped the coach at various places where we were able to take photos, we were proper tourists now, clicking away at every opportunity!

Later as darkness fell, we went up to the top of The Eiffel Tower. We didn't have to queue for long, as Sharon had pre booked the tickets. The night was clear, not a cloud in the sky and we could see the streets of Paris lit up below. It was quite chilly up there, Sharon had to wear her chemo hat to keep her head warm, I also kept putting my arm around her whenever I could as she only had a thin cardigan on and was feeling the cold. As I am writing this, I am thinking that I would do anything now to be able to put my arms around her, I miss that so much.

Whenever I see The Eiffel Tower on TV or in a magazine, I think of that night. In my thoughts, I see Sharon standing there next to a polished brass telescope, and even though she was cold she didn't complain at all. That perfect smile, just melts my heart.

Next day after our continental breakfast we went for a walk around the city and found the Sacre Coeur basilica, where we climbed the steps up to the top. The views were amazing. We also found the spot where the coach driver had stopped so we took a selfie with the tower behind us.

Later that evening there was a special treat for me; Sharon had booked up for us to go for a meal and to see the Moulin Rouge Cabaret Show. We were taken to our table where we had drinks and a very tasty meal. An older couple on the table next to ours, who were British, got talking to us. The lady had noticed that Sharon's hair was short. She said to us, something which I will never forget. She asked if she could hold Sharon's hand, she then looked straight into her eyes and said, "It's ok I know what you are going through, I have also been that person you are today." She commented on how beautiful Sharon looked and what a wonderful couple we made. The kind lady also said that we should enjoy life to the full and make many memories. This lady was so pleased to see us enjoying ourselves, she wanted to take a photo of us with her camera and then with my phone.

I have no idea who this lady was, but thinking about it now, I wonder if she knew what lay ahead for us, was she some kind of psychic?

Sharon and I danced to the live music after our meal, at one point we were the only ones on the dance floor. This was the first time since Sharon had become ill that we were able to dance and you know something, it felt wonderful holding her in my arms. It was then time for the cabaret to begin, which was amazing, we both really enjoyed it.

The next day we had another walk around the city before getting a taxi back to the station for our journey home. I will never forget my birthday trip to Paris, we had so much fun and we certainly made memories which will stay with me for always.

Chapter Forty
The Last Year

I didn't know that I had just one year left with the woman I loved so much. I didn't know that I would be left on my own. Yes, I was concerned, because of what we had been told and what we had read about: "Triple-negative breast cancer differs from other types of breast cancer in that they grow and spread faster, have limited treatment options, and the worse outcome." But we remained focussed and positive; the cancer had been removed in the operation, it hadn't spread to the lymph nodes and the chemotherapy and radiotherapy were to get rid of any rogue cells.

We were focussed on getting fitter and getting stronger; after all we had a cruise booked, Sharon's 50th birthday and our very special wedding day to look forward to. We had everything to live for and we had our future together.

It was September 2017 that we went on a spur of the moment holiday to Fuerteventura, one of the Canary Islands. We had booked up a cheap self-catering apartment in the resort of Caleta De Fuste and it proved to be a well-deserved break for both of us. By now, we were getting fitter and really eating healthily; another reason why we chose self-catering because we didn't want to be tempted by the large quantities of food you get in all-inclusive resorts.

Every morning for the whole week, we set the alarm and were up early and went for walks along the sea path. We would be out for around two hours and on some mornings, we watched the sun rise.

I shall never forget these walks that we did; there is just something special about feeling the warm salty breeze on your face, but most of all it was about being there with my wife to be, and watching this beautiful woman, who just a month earlier, was so fatigued and now she was walking at a pace for miles. I was so proud of her courage, strength and willingness not to give up. Together we were determined and I shall say it again, 'focussed and positive'. In fact, a clinician told me just after Sharon passed, that it was this outlook that we both had and the things we had planned, such as the cruise and wedding, which kept Sharon mentally strong which helped to prolong her life. And yes, I shall say it again. "We had everything to live for and we had our future together."

We spent the days whilst on holiday relaxing on the beach and swimming in the sea. In the evenings, we dressed up in our summer casual clothes and went out for another walk, this time at a much slower pace, and we would eat in different restaurants each night.

One night when we were back at our apartment, we were sitting outside on the patio area and we were talking about holidays and maybe we should book up something for the following year, something else for us to look forward to. So, we looked through the internet and booked a two-week holiday in Hurghada, Egypt.

This was the moment when we pressed the send button, confirming our payment. The holiday was scheduled for July 2018 and by then we would be married.

We arrived home from Fuerteventura on Saturday 16 September 2017. Two days later, on the Monday we were off again, this time to a luxury lodge in Norfolk which had its own private hot tub. We were there for a total of four nights and it was whilst we were there that Sharon received a call from her sister, saying that their dad had sadly passed away. We were just over an hour away from Sharon's sister, so I suggested that I drive there, so that we could comfort each other.

For Sharon to lose both parents in less than five months was very difficult for her and all the family. All I could do was be there for her and support her in whatever way I could. The sad thing was that we had already begun to work out our guests for our wedding, with Sharon's mum and dad joining my parents, bridesmaids and best man on the top table. I still have the piece of A4-sized paper with the original list of guests, handwritten by both Sharon and myself.

It was now the beginning of October 2017; Sharon had been busy making funeral arrangements for her dad and was emotionally exhausted. So, we went away for a mini break to Hayling Island on the South Coast. I know what you are probably all thinking; they are away again! Believe me; it was having these little breaks away, and things planned to look forward to, that helped immensely with both our mental and physical health, and the road to recovery for Sharon from the cancer and its treatment.

Whilst away we did lots of walking and used the gym each morning before breakfast. We downloaded a walk from the internet which took us around the old town of Portsmouth. This was something that we always tried to do wherever we went, because it was a bit like a treasure hunt, and we got to learn about the history and see the sights, which we would have otherwise passed by.

We were staying in a holiday centre which had evening entertainment, and for this weekend it was Queen and Elvis tribute acts. Needless to say, we were up dancing each night and having a great time. I took the next photo just as we got off the dance floor. I love the way Sharon is looking at me.

Back home we were busy planning our wedding; Sharon had chosen the colour scheme for the flowers and bridesmaids' dresses. Together we discussed and decided to have a hog roast carvery in the afternoon, followed by a buffet later in the evening. We booked the caterers for the hog roast and my sister, Janice, kindly offered to do the evening buffet. Being as the wedding was going to be just after Christmas and the new year celebrations, I had the idea of getting a large soup warmer and having hot mulled wine available for our guests. I managed to find a second-hand soup warmer for sale on the internet. So, one afternoon Sharon and I drove around forty miles to collect it.

I will tell you more about our wedding later but first I have our cruise and Sharon's surprise 50th birthday party to talk about, both of which deserve their own chapters.

It was also in late October 2017, when we both went on a week-long physiotherapy course at The Fire Fighters Charity centre in Littlehampton on the south coast. It was here where we met some lovely people, all connected with the UK fire service in one way or another. Each one was there for their own reasons. Sharon immediately felt at ease with everyone and got involved with all the activities that were required. One evening there was a quiz night and I must admit, I am not that good when it comes to quizzes. Sharon on the other hand was top of the class with her answers. I have already mentioned earlier about the work of the charity and how it has helped Sharon, myself and the family. To date they continue to help me and will always be there for me even when I retire from the fire brigade. Thank you to The Fire Fighters Charity.

It was also around the end of October 2017 that Sharon had to go for a mammogram. We were told that from now on, every year around the anniversary of the first diagnosis Sharon would be called for a routine check. As you would expect, we were both very anxious and as I sat in the waiting room, while Sharon was being examined, I found myself looking around at the blue vinyl chairs, I had fingers crossed and I was frantically looking around for something made from wood, so that I could touch it. Crazy superstitions I know, but what else could I do; I certainly wasn't going to start praying, that was of no help whatsoever before.

It was a few days before our cruise when the postman delivered the white NHS letter. I picked it up from the door mat, and gave it to Sharon, I asked if she would like me to open it and read it first. But she said no, we have been through this together, and you are there for me always. So, we sat on the edge of our bed and opened it together, I pulled it from the envelope and unfolded it so that we could both read the results at the same time.

It was all clear, no significant abnormal cells. Well, as you can imagine, we were so happy, we held each other in our arms and we had tears in our eyes. This was just the best news ever, and we spent the next hour calling our families and friends to share our news.

Chapter Forty-One
Cruising the Caribbean

We sat in the departure lounge at Gatwick airport on 4 November 2017, waiting for our flight number to be called and if I was to say we were excited, would be an understatement. The night before we had done what we usually did and stayed in a hotel near to the airport. We boarded the airplane and made ourselves comfortable for the long-haul flight. Next stop sunny Barbados.

As we stepped out of the plane onto the tarmac, the heat hit us, we had planned ahead and packed shorts and summer clothes in our hand luggage. A quick dash to the toilets while on our way to baggage reclaim, and as if by magic, we appeared wearing totally different clothing, thankfully we didn't look all-white like the typical Brit on holiday, because we still had our tans from Fuerteventura.

A small coach took us from the airport to the port where our ship Azura was moored up. I remember watching Sharon's expression on her face as we turned the corner and saw the massive ship for the first time, which was standing so tall and casting a shadow over the warehouses on the quay side. She kept saying, "Wow! look at the size of it." After going through security checks, we were allowed to board and go to our room which had its own private balcony. Our cases were already in the room, so we unpacked and had showers before heading out to explore the ship.

Now, I could spend ages describing the ship in detail and explain everything that we did, every island that we visited and every excursion that we were part of, but instead I will talk about some of the highlights. Not that the whole cruise wasn't fantastic. It really was amazing and we both absolutely loved it.

Our ship was due to sail from Barbados the next day, in the evening, which gave us time to leave the ship and find a beach. We were just smiling all the time, the sand was white in colour and the sea was blue, just like the images that you see on TV commercial adverts, and it was warm too. I am so used to swimming in the North Sea in the UK, which let's just say is rather cold and rather grey in colour. Nearby to where we were laying on the beach was an elderly local man;

he was selling fresh coconuts with the tops chopped off and a drinking straw was placed into it. This was the best coconut water that we had ever had, far better than the watered-down stuff you get in paper cartons back home, this was the real deal, we were in paradise.

One thing about the cruise was the dress code; which was relaxed, apart from four evenings which were spread out over the duration of the cruise, where we had the opportunity to dress up. Sharon had told me that she had never been somewhere where she could dress up in formal clothing, apart from weddings and parties that she had been to and of course the wedding proposal night in New York. When it was these nights, we dressed up and we loved it. I was so proud to be strolling along the decks, holding Sharon's hand and linking arms when we wanted to feel really posh.

We had packed enough 'posh' clothes for each formal night. Sharon was very particular with the colour coordination; making sure that the colours of my ties complemented her dresses and accessories.

One night whilst we were having a drink in one of the lounge areas, Sharon noticed that a man sitting nearby didn't look too well. So here we go again, Essex

Angels to the rescue. I watched the man for a while and Sharon was right he really didn't look well at all, he was white/grey in colour, and was sweating. I approached the man and at first signs, it looked as though he was suffering a heart attack. He was conscious and was talking yet his speech was distorted. By now, a bar tender had noticed the poorly man and telephoned the ship's medical team. I loosened the man's tie and shirt and sat him on the floor and reassured him and his wife. I continued to monitor his condition and kept checking his pulse. Sharon was distracting his wife by talking to her, we didn't want for her to see, should her husband go into cardiac arrest. It wasn't long before the ship's medical team arrived and took him off to the medical centre. Sharon and I carried on with the night, but all the time we wondered how the man was and hoped he was going to be ok.

That night, back in our cabin it took me ages to fall asleep. I was thinking of the man and going over everything that I had done; did I do everything right? Could I have done more to help this man? In my line of work as a fire fighter, after every incident which I attend I always go back through every detail in my thoughts, particularly if it has been a nasty one where someone has died or been injured, be it in a fire or car crash.

I eventually fell asleep, only to be woken up at around 06.30hrs by the ship's public address system, saying 'medical emergency in cabin?' this message was repeated about four times.

I was now thinking that the man who I had helped had possibly died. The day happened to be an at sea day, with no stops. After breakfast, we made our way up to the top deck and found ourselves two sun loungers overlooking the main swimming pool, where the daily entertainment and games would be taking place. About two hours had now passed; we had been in and out of the pool and were sunbathing looking out over the blue seas; when a message from the captain of the ship interrupted the music being played through the speakers positioned around the ship. The message basically said that a medical helicopter was on its way to the ship to take a man who had been taken ill to hospital, and all outside areas including sun decks had to be evacuated. Lots of crew members seemed to appear from nowhere and began stacking up the sun loungers and tables, lashing them down with ropes. They had to prepare for the helicopter to land.

Sharon and I made our way inside and sat in one of the lounge areas, we couldn't even go back to our cabin because we had a balcony. From the window, we watched the helicopter approach and circle the ship before landing.

161

I guess it must have been around an hour and half before we were allowed to go back outside. The captain announced that a man had sadly passed away and that the ship's medical team had done everything that they could for him.

Now you can imagine what I was now thinking, did I do something wrong when I was giving first aid to that man the night before? Not that I doubted my actions at all but I was now going over and over everything that I had done.

It was later that day when we returned from our cabin that a note had been passed under the door, it was a thank you note from the medical team for our actions from the night before, and as a goodwill gesture there was a complimentary meal for two in one of the speciality restaurants. How did they find us? I never gave our names. I can only assume they used the CCTV and identified us from that.

I wanted to put my mind at rest and find out what actually happened to the man I gave first aid to. So, we went to the medical deck and I made myself known to one of the nurses.

It turned out that the man who I thought was having a heart attack and who had died was actually well, he had been suffering from dehydration and after being given some fluids, fully recovered. The nurse thanked us both again for what we had done for this man. Another man did die earlier that day but it wasn't the man I gave first aid to.

I felt relieved that I hadn't done anything wrong and I was happy that the man had made a full recovery. Then I felt sadness for the man who sadly passed and my thoughts turned to his family.

We never saw the man that we helped that night. It's a big ship with lots of passengers.

We did book up our free meal for the next evening at the Indian Restaurant and whilst we were there, we raised our glasses and paid respects to the man who sadly died.

Whilst on our cruise of the Caribbean we visited many islands and got to experience many wonderful things with the excursions that we had booked.

One of those places was Amber Cove, Dominican Republic. We arrived early in the morning and as we disembarked from the ship, we were greeted by locals playing musical instruments and welcoming us. After walking through the terminal, cleverly designed to take you past souvenir and expensive clothes shops, we reached a row of waiting coaches.

The excursion that we had booked for today was a boat trip to 'Paradise Island'. Our coach took us to a beautiful beach with soft white sand, we had about two hours here, lunch was included and we had time to swim in the crystal-clear sea and relax in the hammocks positioned on the beach. Ok, I am going to be honest, I really struggled getting into the hammock, after four attempts and getting covered in sand where I kept falling out of it, I decided to opt for the more comfortable double sun lounger. However, Sharon gracefully managed to climb into it without being tipped out.

The next part of the excursion was a speed boat ride which took us to the 'Paradise Island'; this being a naturally formed sand island, about the size of half a football pitch, surrounded by the blue seas. Stood on the island were some roughly built wooden huts belonging to the various tour operators, in the huts were life jackets and snorkel and masks. We had taken our own full-face mask and snorkel, we both found these so much better than the traditional type. The beautiful coloured fish here were amazing, we were allowed thirty minutes in the water here before returning back to the sand island for fruit punch.

We only had limited amount of time on the island so we made the most of the fruit punch and soaked up the sun's rays.

On the way back to the mainland, our speed boat driver suddenly turned the boat towards a small inlet, and travelling quite fast we entered a mangrove forest. We had no idea that this was included in the excursion, I am so glad it was. It was amazing, the boat weaved in and out of the small channels, the roots of the mangroves were just inches away from the side of the boat.

Like I said, we did many excursions whilst on our cruise but this was one of our favourites. On another boat trip, we did stop at a secluded beach with white sand and clear waters, we spent a lot of time here, snorkelling and exploring the caves. In the next photo, you see Sharon in one of those caves, I wonder what thoughts were going through her mind. It was one of those special moments that I am glad I captured.

Every time the ship left a port, which was in the evening as the sun began to set, there was a sail-away party up on the pool deck. One evening that I shall never forget was when they put union jack flags everywhere and gave out garlands to wear around our necks. We were on a P & O cruise so it was very British; we were singing and dancing and waving our flags.

Whilst on the cruise it was Sharon's 50th birthday, 17 November 2017. By now, we had been to many beautiful islands, sun bathed on secluded beaches and swum in crystal clear waters. Our last stop was back where we started, Barbados, and we arrived in the port in the late afternoon of 16 November. We were scheduled to leave the ship for our journey home on the 18th. This gave us a full day and night in Barbados on Sharon's birthday.

For the whole duration of the cruise, our room had been serviced by a very friendly man called Leo. I had planned ahead by packing birthday banners and balloons, which were hidden in my travel case. So, I asked Leo if he could decorate our room whilst we were having dinner on the 16th, Sharon had no idea. Ok, so I know some of you may be thinking, why do it on the day before her birthday? Well; Barbados time is four hours behind UK time, so my plan was to go back to our room after our evening meal which would be around 21.00hrs. In the UK, it would actually be 01.00hrs in the morning of the 17th, so technically it was actually Sharon's birthday.

Everything went to plan; Sharon opened our cabin door and went in first, birthday banners were stuck on the walls, balloons had been blown up and placed on the bed, and a bottle of champagne, chilling in a silver ice bucket, was left on the dressing table.

I had also asked Leo to take a present and card which I had hidden in my case and place it on the bed. Sure enough, surrounded by the balloons was the gift box covered in bright pink glitter which sparkled. Sharon was so excited and in shock as she wasn't expecting all of this. She sat on the bed and opened the card first, followed by taking the lid off the gift box to reveal another card sitting on top of some shredded pink tissue paper. I said to open that card first and read aloud what I had written inside; these were the words

"To my darling Sharon, to celebrate your 50th birthday I have chosen a little trip. I know that you like fire and ice! So, I reckon that this last two weeks have been the fire, (the hot part) and the cold part is; well, you are a great mum and where do all good mums go?"

Sharon replied with the answer 'Iceland'. For those of you who don't know, in the UK, there is a TV commercial advertising a supermarket of the same name and they use the slogan; *'That's why mums go to Iceland'*.

Under the tissue paper was a travel guide of Iceland and beneath that two A4 size photos that I had printed at home on photo paper. The first was The Blue Lagoon and the other was a photo of the Northern Lights. It was then when I told Sharon about the excursions that I had booked. For the purpose of this book, I will tell you readers about the trip to Iceland and the excursions a bit later.

Sharon had tears in her eyes and was overwhelmed as she gave me a big hug and thanked me.

It was now the morning of Sharon's birthday, 17 November 2017; today we had two excursions booked. After breakfast, we disembarked from the ship, and met with our tour guide and waiting mini bus, which took us out of the cruise terminal to a marina about five minutes away. It was here where we boarded a boat with other passengers which was going to take us to an area where we had the opportunity to swim amongst wild turtles.

We had our full-face mask, snorkel and fins with us which proved to be one of the best things that we had packed in our cases, as we used them a lot.

There were a lot of people in the water and no sign of any turtles. Sharon looked disappointed after we had been in the water for around twenty minutes and still hadn't seen anything which looked like a turtle. I suggested that we swim away from the other people and it was then that we caught a glimpse of one. Well, what happened next was amazing, I was filming underwater and Sharon just took off, swimming as fast as she could and caught up with the turtle. The beautiful creature must have known it was Sharon's birthday as it kept swimming right up to her and circled her for about five minutes. It was a special moment which bought tears to my eyes. I captured the moment when Sharon appeared from underneath the water, the look of joy and happiness on her face just made me really emotional. In fact, I had to get back on board the boat for a while to compose myself. I was just so happy that Sharon had experienced this on her birthday.

I apologise for the quality of the photo; it is a screen shot taken from my underwater video.

And this is Sharon's Turtle. The date in the top left corner reads 2017/11/17 time 09.42:59.

We got back to the ship in the early afternoon, where we had a chance to freshen up and relax on the sun loungers for a couple of hours before we had to get ready.

Our next excursion was a sunset cruise on a large catamaran. We set sail and cruised along the shore line towards the sunset. Quietly, I pointed out to the crew that it was Sharon's birthday, and it wasn't long into the cruise that an announcement was made for Sharon to go to the on-board bar. A drink was passed to her and everyone sang happy birthday. Other guests on the excursion came up to Sharon and congratulated her. I stood back and watched; it was another emotional moment for me, but this time I kept the tears in.

On deck, we had the perfect spot to watch the golden sun get lower and lower and then slowly disappear, sending an orange glow across the sky. There is something so romantic about watching the sunset, especially when you are experiencing it with someone that you love.

Music was being played through the speakers, there were times when we danced and times when we just stood still and took in the views.

Later that night, back on the ship we had a posh meal out on the deck, overlooking the sea. It was now dark, so we couldn't see much of the sea; however, the moon and stars were so bright; sending shimmering reflections on the gentle ripples, which looked like a million dancing angels.

Sharon's birthday was just what I wanted it to be for her; fun, laughter, happiness and full of love and warmth.

Chapter Forty-Two
Surprise

We got home from our cruise on 19 November 2017, Sharon's family came round to give her birthday presents.

For a few months before, I had been planning a surprise 50th birthday party for Sharon and the date for this was on Saturday 25 November 2017. I had hired the village hall in Margaretting, which is about a five-minute drive from where we lived. I also set up a 'WhatsApp' group and started to contact Sharon's friends via private message through Facebook, giving them my number so that they could join the group.

A good friend of mine who I have known since the CB radio days, when I was around aged fifteen, manages live tribute acts. One of those acts is a Take That tribute. Knowing that Sharon is a fan and had been to see the real band in concert a few times, I asked her during a telephone call, if she could provide a Take That tribute for the night. Unfortunately, the group were already booked, however she could provide a Gary Barlow tribute and he would be able to sing all the Take-That hits. I was happy with this and the Gary Barlow tribute was booked for the night.

The village hall had a bar, so drinks were taken care of, it was just the food now to sort out. For weeks, I was ringing around different catering firms and they were either fully booked or extremely overpriced. So, I chose to let everyone know that if they wanted food; to bring their own. A few days before the surprise party, Sharon's daughter stepped in and said that she would be happy to prepare a buffet. So, café was straight back on the 'WhatsApp' group and told everyone not to bring their own food as a buffet would be provided.

So how was I going to get Sharon to the hall on the night? Well, I had a plan, you already know how much I like a plan. On the actual date of the party, 25th November, I was due to be at work on day shift. I had already booked this day as leave but didn't tell Sharon. What I said was that on the night of the 25th, when I get home from work, we were going out for a meal with the rest of the family, like we had done on previous birthdays.

The morning of the party came, and I was up early as if I was going to work. We had breakfast together and I even had my uniform on. I gave Sharon a kiss and a hug and said I would see her in the evening and asked that she could be ready for 19.30hrs, as I was hoping to get another fire fighter to do an early relief for me. All this being a little white lie. It was 07.30hrs when I left for 'work', as I was driving out of our road, I thought where do I go now? I hadn't planned this bit! So, I drove to a cafe and had two teas and two milky coffees all in the space of about two hours. In the car, I changed out of my uniform and into jeans and t shirt. Around 10.00hrs I drove into Chelmsford, and found a card shop to buy birthday banners and balloons, so that I could decorate the hall later that day.

Whilst having another tea, and this time, a salmon and cream cheese bagel in a quaint tea room, I had a thought: I knew my friend will be providing the Gary Barlow tribute act, and also said that she would be happy to have music being played during sets. But I thought it would also be good to have a disco as well. So, yes you guessed right, in between more teas and more coffees and lots of toilet breaks I surfed the internet in search of local DJ's. It was very short notice and most were busy but eventually, I found a DJ in a nearby town who would be willing to do the disco that evening

The keys for the hall were available for me to collect at 17.00hrs. A couple of Sharon's friends came along to help me decorate the hall, which was really helpful as I had lots of balloons and banners to put up, as well as setting up the tables and chairs for the guests. Fortunately, I was able to have a shower at the hall and get changed into my suit before all the guests arrived, and by 19.30hrs the DJ had turned up and set up his equipment on stage. The Gary Barlow tribute, had arrived and was keeping out of sight, this not only was going to be a surprise for Sharon, but also for everyone. Sharon's daughter had arrived with trays of food and a beautiful birthday cake, which was all set up along the length of four tables towards the back of the hall. Everyone who had been invited was there and getting in the party spirit. It was now time that I left to go and pick up Sharon. We returned back at the hall at 19.50hrs.

The lights to the hall were turned on the same time that Sharon came through the doors, so that she could see everyone, party poppers with silver-coloured streamers were being set off. Everyone was shouting "SURPRISE" and coming up to kiss and hug Sharon. The song, 'Celebration' by the band Kool and the Gang, was being played by the DJ. Sharon was just totally surprised and overwhelmed and she had tears in her eyes, as did I. To be honest I think a lot of people were emotional, after all that Sharon had been through, and now here she was, looking and feeling fit, healthy and strong again. And I am not just saying it, she did look absolutely stunning.

The lights were dimmed again as Sharon made her way around the family and friends. My mum and dad, and my children, Jason and Mia, were there with their partners as well as my sister Angela and her family, sadly my other sister, Janice couldn't make it that night. All of Sharon's family were there apart from her brother, Steve and his wife.

The DJ kept everyone dancing for the first hour until it was time for 'Gary Barlow' to make an appearance. He made his way on stage to his own backing introduction and began singing 'Greatest Day' with the opening lyrics being; *"Today this could be, the greatest day of our lives."* He was amazing sounded just like the real Gary Barlow, not only when he sang but also when he spoke, wishing Sharon a Happy Birthday. Everyone was up on the dance floor, clapping and cheering; it was almost like being at a real concert.

The whole night was a complete success; it was a total surprise for Sharon which is what I wanted. The DJ was really good and interacted with everyone and not once was the dance floor empty. The buffet that Lauren had prepared was lovely and there was plenty of it.

'Gary Barlow' did two sets which were just brilliant, he sang a lot of the famous Take-That songs and there was one song he sang which was really special. He called Sharon up onto the stage and asked her to sit on a chair. He then got down on one knee and sang Take That's version of the Bee Gees hit, 'How Deep is Your Love'. Well, Sharon had her very own 'Gary Barlow' singing to her, she loved it and so did everyone there. Nowadays if I hear this song, be it by the Bee Gees or Take That, I think of that night and how happy Sharon and everyone was.

Chapter Forty-Three
Iceland

Like I said earlier, Sharon's 50th birthday present from me was a trip to Iceland. It was on 18 December 2017, around midday, when we arrived in Reykjavik. That night we had a cruise booked to see the Northern Lights; unfortunately, the weather was so bad with snow showers that the trip was cancelled. I had to check the website on the next day to see if it was going to go ahead then. Sadly, the weather the whole time whilst we were in Iceland was bad, and the cruise didn't go ahead, and we never got to see the Northern Lights. I know Sharon really would have loved to experience them and I feel sad that she never got that chance. I intend to one day travel to see the lights, maybe Norway, and when I do, it will certainly be very emotional.

In the evening, we walked around Reykjavik in search for somewhere reasonably priced to eat. We eventually found a bar that was doing an offer on a drink, burger and fries, which was still overpriced but nowhere near as dear as the meals in the local restaurants. We ate in the same bar on the other two nights of our trip. Walking around the capital, seeing the Christmas lights and decorated trees with the snow falling, made it look and feel so magical.

The next day's trip was to the Blue Lagoon, a geothermal spa, our coach picked us up at 08.00hrs, and it was still dark. Daylight hours during the winter months in Iceland are very few.

We both absolutely loved the Blue Lagoon, we stayed in the milky blue hot water for most of the day. The temperature of the water ranges from 37 to 38 degree Celsius. We had applied silica mud face packs which was so much fun.

At one point whilst in the lagoon, the wind picked up and it began to snow, feeling it sting our faces was quite invigorating. The rest of our bodies were nice and warm in the water.

I had also booked for us to do a snowmobile ride on a glacier for the next day. Getting there was fun, we had to board a giant snow truck with huge wheels which had snow chains on. Being as Sharon and I were first in the queue we got the best seats, on the top deck at the front. It was a bumpy journey along the deeply covered snow roads and onto the glacier. Sharon was so much better at driving the snowmobile than me. It was so cold my fingers were numb which was entirely my fault. I had taken a spare pair of firefighting gloves with me, thinking they would keep my hands warm. I was wrong; they are good at keeping heat out, such as in a fire, but in the freezing cold they are useless. Sharon was fine, she had the correct gloves. So maybe this is why she was a better driver than me!

Even though we never got to see the Northern Lights, we had an amazing time and to experience the snow and to watch Sharon make snow angels, was just perfect.

Chapter Forty-Four
Last Christmas

Sharon had been busy making table decorations and a table plan for our wedding. She had collected empty jars which she decorated with lace ribbon and put artificial flowers in them. I remember coming home from work one evening, finding her in the kitchen with her arts and crafts things, making the table plan. Sharon had also joined a Facebook wedding group, and had bought small bird cage centre pieces for each table, which looked amazing, especially when Sharon dressed them up.

I was on duty on Christmas Eve night and Christmas day night. Oh, the joys of working for a 24-hour emergency service. If I knew that this was going to be Sharon's last ever Christmas, I would not have worked at all.

On Christmas morning, I got home from night shift at around 10.00hrs. Sharon was there waiting with open arms and a cuppa tea. We sat for a while listening to festive songs while we exchanged presents. My sister, Angela, invited us over for dinner, which was really nice as my mum and dad were also there, as well as my brother-in-law's parents. We had an amazing dinner and also celebrated my dad's birthday.

We played the after-dinner mint chocolate game; you balance the chocolate on your forehead with your head tilted back, you then have to bring your head back to its normal position and catch the chocolate in your mouth before it falls. Sharon always participated in fun games. Unfortunately, because I was on duty that night, we had to leave in the early evening to give me a chance to take Sharon home and for me to get to work, before start of shift at 20.00hrs.

The following day, Boxing Day, was when we had a family meal at a local pub in Chelmsford, it was really a nice idea for Sharon's family and my children and their partners to all be together.

The festive season was lovely and even though I had to work, we still managed to see our families which was very important to us. While we were celebrating Christmas, Sharon and I were busting with excitement about our wedding and the honeymoon.

The days after Christmas we just ran through the final plans for our wedding. Sharon and her son made the mulled wine and filled up four five litre plastic containers, which were going to be warmed up on the stove on the day and kept warm in the soup warmer. On one of my duty days, I took the dance floor into work to set it up in the appliance bay. Oh, that's right the dance floor, well I shall tell you the story of the dance floor:

Our wedding venue, The Reid Rooms, is exactly what it says in its name. It is made up of various rooms, the dining room being the largest, which is where you have the tables set up for the meal and speeches. Just off this room through glazed double doors is a lounge area, with a log burner and soft seating made up of armchairs and sofas. A grand piano stands in the corner. Then through another set of doors, on the opposite side of the dining room, is an area which has the toilets, and then another door which leads through to the bar with wooden dance floor. It is here where on previous weddings the disco is set up.

Well, when Sharon and I first viewed the venue, I said that it would feel strange that after our meal and speeches that we would all have to go through to the bar. It would be a shame to leave the nicely decorated tables behind, plus there would be no room for seating. I wanted for all the guests to be together. After two further visits to the venue and hours of discussion, we both agreed to keep everything in the largest room. The only trouble being that the floor had carpet on it. I was now on a mission to hire or purchase a dance floor, so, out came the laptop and I eventually found a second-hand portable dance floor for sale, which I bought. I had to sand each panel down to make it look new again, and had to apply four coats of floor varnish. I even bought multi coloured rope lighting which I put around the edge. On the morning of our wedding, it was going to be my job, with the help of my best man, to put it down and connect it all together. So, this is why I took it to work with me, as a rehearsal, to make sure I knew exactly what to do.

Sharon had a countdown app on her phone and in our kitchen was a board, where we wrote how many days it was until we say 'I do'. The photo below was taken the day before our special day, 23 hours 29 minutes and 6 seconds to be precise, before Sharon walked down the aisle.

Chapter Forty-Five
Our Wedding Day

Before I tell you about our special day, let me tell you about the important people who helped with the planning and had important roles to play on the day itself.

When Sharon and I changed our wedding plans, to getting married in the UK, Sharon said that she wasn't too bothered about having bridesmaids. Now, obviously, it was going to be Sharon's decision entirely, but I thought that it would be nice if she did have one or two. So, after a few weeks of me dropping it in to our conversations, Sharon made the choice to have her daughter and my daughter as bridesmaids. She also chose to have her granddaughter as flower girl and grandson as page boy. Together, we chose both Sharon's sons to be ushers on the day. Sharon chose her brother to walk with her down the aisle and to formally give her away.

As I mentioned earlier, Sharon sadly lost both her mum and dad in 2017. I feel sad that they were not with us in person on our day, however they were definitely there in spirit. I managed to get two heart shaped memorial bouquet charms and had Sharon's mum and dad's wedding photos put in them. Attached to the ring is a separate heart engraved with the words, "Always in my heart."

I wanted Sharon's parents to be with us and particularly with Sharon on our special day.

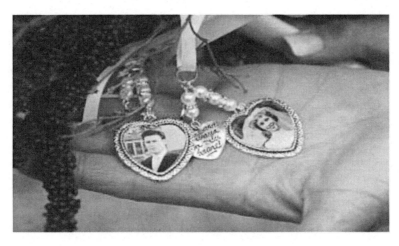

I was lucky to still have both my parents and it was an honour to have them sitting on our top table.

As for me, choosing my best man wasn't difficult. I have plenty of friends and colleagues but haven't really got a best mate, or drinking buddy. And even if I did have, my choice would have been the same. I chose my son, Jason, to be my best man. Jason has always stood by me and has always been there for me, we may not be drinking buddies but we are best mates and we certainly know a good cafe or two.

Sharon's sister and my sister were to be our formal witnesses and my other sister Janice kindly offered to supply and prepare the evening buffet.

Every single family member or friend who celebrated our wedding day were so important to us because they helped make the day special in every way.

Traditionally, the future husband and wife should not spend the night together before their wedding. So, in the afternoon of 4 January 2018, Jason brought Mia over to us. Sharon spent the night at home with her bridesmaids. Jason and I went to Angela's house, had a Chinese takeaway meal and spent the night there.

Next morning, our wedding day 5 January 2018, Jason and I were up early, we had to go back home and pick up my van, which I had loaded up the day before with the dance floor, mulled wine and table decorations.

The wedding venue, The Reid Rooms, also has an old farmhouse within the grounds; just a short two-minute walk to the ceremony room and barn where the reception was. In the house, there is a bridal suite and other rooms available for guests to stay. This was where Sharon and I and the immediate family got ready and spent the wedding night.

Jason and I got to the venue around 08.00hrs, we set up the dance floor and placed all the table decorations in an area, ready for the staff to dress the tables. We then headed off at 10.00hrs, to have a full English breakfast in a nearby country pub.

It was around 11.30hrs when we got back to the wedding venue. Sharon and the bridesmaids were not far behind us, and Jason made sure that I didn't see Sharon at all.

When Sharon was safely in the bridal suite, Jason took me to his room where I began to get ready.

Jason helping me and Mia helping with Sharon's make-up.

The best way to describe the actual ceremony is to tell you my feelings and what I saw as if it was happening now, and believe me I relive that special day over and over again in my thoughts. So, here goes…

It's now 13.45hrs, all the guests have arrived and are sitting in the ceremony room, a beautiful quaint room with exposed beams with twinkling fairy lights wrapped around. Standing in the doorway with Jason, looking down the length of the room I can see the table at the end, standing behind are the two ladies, the registrars, who will be performing the service. On the table is the beautiful silk flower arrangement that Sharon had arranged to have made. (This was later moved to the top table in the main dining room). To my right is the violinist that I had arranged as a surprise for Sharon.

(When we were planning our wedding, we spoke about what music Sharon was going to walk down the aisle to and what other songs would be played whilst signing the register, and then the exit music. We didn't want any actual songs with lyrics being sung, we wanted to have instrumental only. Sharon had heard the violin versions of our chosen songs and loved them. So, I downloaded them on my phone and the plan was to get someone on the day to play the said songs through the speaker system within the room. Well, instead I searched the internet and found a local violinist who would be willing to play our songs at the ceremony, and then afterwards whilst reception drinks were being poured. I also printed off the lyrics to the exit song and had the ushers give these out. Again, Sharon had no idea about this).

Jason and I walked down to the registrars, stopping on the way saying hello to family and friends. I'm not feeling nervous at all, I'm feeling very emotional though. It's ok though, I have two hankies in my pocket, one for tears and one for a snotty nose. Deep breaths Russell, come on, pull yourself together. It's now 14.00hrs.

I can hear the violinist start to play *'Can't Help Falling in Love with You'*. (The Elvis Presley song). Everyone is asked to stand for the Bridal Party. I can see the flower girl, being helped by the page boy, sprinkling petals as they walk down the aisle. My eyes though, are drawn towards Sharon, her brother is holding her hand. Now I can really feel myself getting choked up, a quick hankie moment to wipe my eyes. There she is, my beautiful wife to be, looking stunning in an amazing elegant wedding dress, with a white feather shawl draped across her shoulders. I see her look surprised as she notices the violinist playing. Sharon's smile and her energy just radiates, filling the room with warmth and happiness as she walks down the aisle towards me. The bridesmaids, who were following behind take their seats. Sharon leans towards me and we kiss and our hands find each other, and I tell her that she looks absolutely stunning.

The registrar welcomes everyone and the ceremony begins; I am holding Sharon's hands and gazing into her eyes. It's me who has to repeat the vows and promises first, and as you would imagine I am very emotional as I say these words:

"As I take you to be my wife.
I promise to Love you.
To honour and respect you.
I will stand by you.
And be true to you always.
I will care for you.
Laugh with you when you are happy.
Comfort you when you are sad.
Whatever life may bring,
I will always Love you."

I take a deep breath and wipe my eyes; it's now Sharon's turn and she speaks so calmly; the soft tone of her voice gently bouncing off every surface, filling the quiet room for everyone to hear.

The next part of the ceremony is the giving and exchanging of rings. It's my turn first to place the ring on Sharon's finger which slides on perfectly, unlike mine which needed a little bit of my saliva to moisten my finger to help it on its way. As we both push the rings on, we say the following words:

"I give you this ring, as a token of our marriage and as a lasting reminder of the promises we have made here today."

As I'm writing these words for you all to read, looking down at the keyboard, I catch a glimpse of Sharon's wedding ring. It now permanently hangs on a chain around my neck, and it shall always be a lasting reminder. Not just of our wedding day and those promises that we made, but of my beautiful wife who once wore it on her finger and of all the happiness and love that she brought to my life. I still remember how happy we were when we went to the jewellers to buy her ring, coincidently the date was 5 January 2017, the year before.

(I need to take a break; I'm struggling to see the laptop keys through my tears.)

We have now both exchanged rings and the registrar reads the following statement;

"So, Russell and Sharon having consented in law before your witnesses and guests here today, to accept the state of matrimony, and by virtue of the vows you have made, and the giving and receiving of a ring, it's my pleasure to announce that you are now Husband and Wife."

Sharon begins to jump for joy as we turn and face each other, she reaches up and puts her arms around my neck as my arms naturally wrap around her back and waist. Pulling each other closer we kiss, I then raise my hands above my head with open palms, Sharon does the same and our hands meet, as we join together for a 'high ten'.

We now have to sign the official Wedding certificate and are joined by our witnesses, Sharon's sister and my sister. The violinist begins to play our other choices of music whilst we sit at the table; *'Signed, Sealed, delivered'*, (by Stevie Wonder), which was followed by *'All of Me'*, (by John Legend). However, I'm not paying much attention to the music, I'm just fixated on Sharon and signing the certificate, as the guests come forward and take photos.

It's now time for us to walk down the aisle as husband and wife, and as we stand together, hand in hand the registrar asks everyone to stand as we slowly begin the walk. The violinist plays our exit song; *All You Need is Love* (by The Beatles) and as planned everyone picks up the song lyrics I printed off and begins to sing. My wife and I join in as we walk past our cheering guests and make our way outside, across the courtyard and into the reception room. Our guests join us for drinks, (the warm mulled wine is a big hit), and as we make our way around the room, we are congratulated by everyone. The violinist has now set up opposite the bar and is playing a selection of music.

As it was winter, and the daylight begins to fade around 16.00hrs, our photographer was keen to get us outside to take photos while the sun was still shining. First of all, Sharon and I were taken around the grounds, where a number of photos were taken followed by group photos in the courtyard. Every photo that was taken on our special day is so special to me and I shall cherish them always.

After the photos were taken, it was time for everyone to take their seats in the main room. Sharon and I had to wait until we were formally asked to enter the room, and when we did everyone clapped and cheered. We made our way to the top table and took our seats.

The caterers gave the go ahead for us to make our way to the hog roast which was set up in an adjoining room, top table first followed by the rest of the tables one by one. Everyone commented on how nice the meal was and it made a pleasant change from a traditional wedding sit down meal.

Around half hour after everyone had finished their desserts it was time for the speeches. Jason, my best man stood up and introduced each speaker, Sharon's brother was first. Next it was my dad, who gave a lovely speech, welcoming Sharon into the Webb family. Then Sharon's grandson stood up and said a few words, which was a total surprise to us. Next up was my best man/son, Jason whose speech was really good, he shared stories of fun times that we had when my children were younger. He even told the story which I had told them a few times.

"When I was a child in the infants' school, at the end of the day the music trolley was wheeled in by the teacher, the trolley had drums, a guitar, tambourines and various other instruments. Somehow, I never got one of the good things, I always ended up with the triangle. While all the other kids were playing their instruments, in time with the teacher playing the piano, I had to wait ages for my turn to ding the triangle, but only allowed to do it once."

Jason then presented me with a triangle, which I was able to use later when the band was playing.

Next it was my turn. I still have my speech in the same folder which I used on the day. So, here it is for you all to read, I will start from after I had done all the thankyous.

My Wedding speech.
About six months ago, I began to search Google and
YouTube for grooms' speeches, to get some inspiration.
After many hours of reading and watching, it soon became
apparent that the words were not suited for me. So, I have
decided to speak in my own words, which come from my
heart…

We first met three years and four months ago, many thanks to internet dating. That's right, I used to spend many days and night trawling the pages of Plenty of Fish. I went on the odd date or two or three or four, maybe five or six!

I made some silly choices back then, but there are two people in this room who always stood by me and never judged me, even when I made bad decisions. Those two people are my children, Jason and Mia. Thank you so much. I love you both.

My dad always used to say to me. "One day Russell, you will meet the perfect woman who will be right in every way."

Now on one not so busy night at the fire station, Sharon's photo and profile flashed up on my phone.

After a few messages, we exchanged numbers and spoke the very next morning. A few days later we met in a coffee shop in Stock near Billericay and had our first date on the same day in Southend, where we sat on Russell's bench overlooking the sea and eating a Rossi Ice cream.

Wow! I was well and truly blown away by your looks, kindness and personality. In fact, I had finally found someone who knocked me off my feet. My perfect catch.

So, Dad your wise words really did come true that first time I set eyes on Sharon.

Over the last three years and four months, we have been to some amazing places and had wonderful holidays. But Sharon, nothing compares to the warmth I feel every time I look into your eyes and see your beautiful smile.

Now this last year has been filled with many emotions. Sharon, firstly had the cancer diagnosis, which came to a massive shock and blow to us all. Just a month before that we had booked a cruise and had planned to marry onboard the ship, alone.

I suppose the only good thing to come out of the diagnosis was that we both decided to change our plans and marry here instead, so that we can have our family and friends with us on this special day.

Sharon's treatment finished in July, just six months ago. At that point, Sharon was tired, weak and exhausted. It was at that point that we both decided to get fit again, a life style change.

Sharon, I have every bit of respect for you, you joined a gym. You got up early to do Joe Wicks workouts in front of the TV, and we go on walks.

Between the two of us we have lost an amazing six stone in weight, most of that belonging to me.

I'm pleased to announce that Sharon's recent scan results came back as normal. meaning Sharon is cancer free.

Sharon, I have never ever met anyone who is as strong, brave and positive as you are. You always put others first. A fine example of this is that you always made the time to visit your mum in between chemotherapy treatments.

Even when you were feeling your worst and very poorly you always greeted her with that warm smile of yours and your mum was so pleased to see you.

This brings me to Sharon's mum and dad who both sadly passed away last year. They were both lovely people, I'm glad I was able to meet them. I shall miss having them as my mother and father-in-law. Please raise your glasses and pay tribute to Sharon's mum and dad.

We all know someone who can't be here for whatever reason. For me, it's my brother, Steven who died from cancer many years ago. So, please raise your glasses and shout out their names. Thankyou.

Now, on a lighter note, a bit later Sharon and I will be doing our first dance as Husband and Wife. The song is an Elvis Presley song, which he used to sing during his Vegas years. (No, I'm not going to change into a jump suit).

In fact, Elvis always sang this song as his final song, at all of his concerts.

Well Sharon, I can assure you that this is not our finale. It is however just the beginning of what I promise will be an exciting, amazing, wonderful and loving marriage for always.

Here's to my beautiful wife, Sharon.

I LOVE YOU TO BITS.

As I rewrite my words, I am drawn to the part where I say Sharon is cancer free. This is what we both thought especially when the mammogram showed no abnormal cells. However, it was highly likely that cancer cells were elsewhere in her body. I shall talk more about this later.

We had our first dance to Elvis Presley's *'Can't Help Falling in Love with You'*, superbly sung by the male vocalist from the band.

The rest of the evening was just brilliant, we cut the wedding cake and indulged in the wonderful buffet that my sister, Janice, had provided. The dance floor was packed right through to the last song. Sharon and I danced all night and we even joined the band to sing 'Suspicious Minds', another Elvis song.

We spent our Wedding night in the Bridal Suite in the farmhouse. Next morning, we had a full English breakfast waiting for us and were joined by everyone who had also stayed in the farmhouse. Sharon and I sat at the head of the long table on a double chair. Our breakfast was served on heart shaped plates.

To sum up our wedding; it was absolutely wonderful in every way. The best thing about our wedding was my beautiful wife.

The memories of our wedding shall stay with me for always, as will all the other special memories that I have of my lovely Sharon.

Chapter Forty-Six
Honeymoon

Our honeymoon began on 8 January 2018, when we left home and made our way to Gatwick Airport; we had booked a room in a nearby hotel, our flight to Jamaica was the next morning.

Neither of us had been to Jamaica before, the resort where we were staying had been recommended by one of Sharon's friends, which turned out to be an excellent recommendation.

We were staying in Runaway Bay at the Luxury Bahia Principe resort. Our room was massive, it had a white four-poster bed, a separate area which had a dining table with two white wooden chairs and a comfortable sofa. The bathroom was huge; his and hers sinks and a walk-in shower, big enough for the two of us, and there was the jacuzzi bath which had a window above, which looked out into the main room. I thought this strange at first as I'm sure Sharon wouldn't have wanted to see me sitting on the loo, then we realised there was a curtain which could be pulled across. The balcony was just as large with our own sunbeds which overlooked the private beach which we had access to, the views from our room were amazing.

The resort was massive and we had a choice of themed restaurants, some were buffet style and others were more formal and had table service. At breakfast, we would opt for the buffet and in the evening, we dressed up and dined in the posher ones, with the table service; after all we were on our honeymoon and we both felt very posh. Lunch times we would go to the more relaxed open-air restaurant by the beach, and it was here where we both developed the taste for Jerk Chicken, often going back to the BBQ for a second helping.

The private beach was just wonderful, soft white sand and crystal-clear warm sea, where we would spend ages just relaxing, sunbathing and swimming. We also took our snorkels away with us, there were so many beautiful coloured fish which always swam around Sharon. This may have had something to do with the bread rolls that she had taken from breakfast and was feeding the fish with.

There were times when we sat together on the sand with the sea gently breaking over our legs, we laughed and we talked, and sometimes we just looked and took it all in. On occasions, Sharon just went to the water's edge on her own to cool down. On one occasion, I remember watching my beautiful wife and thinking to myself, *How lucky I was and then suddenly it hit me! I had one of those bad thoughts of mine; would she be here in five years and what would I do if the cancer came back?* I was so happy and so in love and that thought of losing Sharon was very frightening. I took a deep breath, shook my head to get rid of those thoughts and got up and walked over to Sharon and took the next photo. Seeing her lovely smile makes everything perfect.

Whilst in Jamaica, we booked up an excursion to see Dunn's River Falls. We were met outside the reception by our mini bus driver, who took us to a nearby harbour where we boarded a boat.

The boat trip took us around the bay and dropped anchor, where we were able to snorkel for a while. The only way to access the falls is from the beach, so the boat took us further around the bay to where the falls cascade into the sea. Now, we had no idea what we would be doing, we thought that we would just be viewing a water fall from a viewing area. We were wrong. You start at the bottom and you actually walk up the River Falls in groups, one behind the other. The fresh water is cold and exhilarating. The rocks and boulders are slippery at times but the guides took us up the safest route.

It was one of the most amazing things that we had done, there was even a part where we were allowed to slide down the rocks straight into a pool of water. You were only meant to do it once but Sharon sneaked back into the line of waiting people and had another go.

Another excursion that we did was to swim with dolphins, which was something that we both always wanted to do. At Dolphin Cove, there were other exotic animals to see and interact with. We stopped at an area with beautifully coloured parrots, and as you can see from the next photo, Sharon handled them so gently and they soon took to her, repeating every word that she said.

In the pool, our guide introduced us to the dolphins, they were named Mitch and Sky. We were told to swim to the other side of the pool and float on our fronts, we then felt each dolphin touch our feet and push us along and out of the water. Another manoeuvre involved us holding onto their fins and they both pulled us along the water, fast!

Swimming with the dolphins and climbing Dunn's River Falls, were both amazing things to do, and I am so glad that we experienced them together on our honeymoon.

Apart from acquiring a taste for Jerk chicken, we also developed a taste for Bob Marley music, we didn't have much choice, because it's all that was played everywhere. I mean the resort had his music piped through every outdoor speaker. In the taxis and excursion buses, Bob was being played. Nowadays, whenever I hear reggae music sung by Bob Marley, I think of our honeymoon and for a moment or two, I am transported back to laying with my wife on the white/golden sand, feeling the warm sea around us.

Our honeymoon in Jamaica was to be the last time that we were abroad and the last time that we flew on an airplane together.

Chapter Forty-Seven
New Home

Whilst on our honeymoon we spoke lots about our future and what we both wanted, we were making mental plans of the places we wanted to travel, and plans of where we wanted to live. The plan was to move home locally and stay there for four years until I retired from the fire brigade. We would then move further away in the countryside, where house rentals are cheaper and then spend time travelling the world, enjoying each other and making memories. Sadly, we only managed to do the first part of our plans.

It was at the start of February 2018, when we found a lovely cottage on the other side of Writtle, which was up for rent. It was really quaint, a small cosy lounge, a large kitchen/dining room, two good sized bedrooms, a study, garage and huge garden.

Also, during February, Sharon was having a lot of pain in her left arm and elbow, her doctor gave her some pain relief and treated her for tennis elbow.

We moved into our new home on 1 March 2018, snow still lay on the ground in places. We felt so at home in our little cottage, we loved the fact that it had a large garden and were looking forward to spending a lot of time out there. In the evenings after dinner, we would sit in the lounge with our feet up and look through charts, trying to pick out the colours that we wanted to paint the walls.

Sharon was also getting lots of pain in her back, which we put down to the new bed and mattress that we had got. At night while in bed, she just couldn't get comfortable.

Whilst on the honeymoon, I noticed that Sharon had a very slight cough, nothing persistent and she managed it by taking a cough mixture at night.

The cough was not getting any worse but it had been lingering on and I insisted that Sharon should make an appointment to see her doctor. It must have been around 12 March that Sharon went to see her doctor who arranged for her to have a chest x-ray, to see if everything was as it should be.

Chapter Forty-Eight
Our Worst Fears

This brings me to 21 March 2018, just three weeks after moving into our home.

I was up early and getting ready to go to work. Sharon was still asleep, I took her a cup of tea, gave her a kiss on the cheek and whispered 'I love you', then headed back down stairs to have my breakfast. It was time for me to leave and I was just about to go out of the back door when Sharon walked into the kitchen, looking white as a sheet and eyes filled with tears. She looked straight at me with the look of fear on her face and said that the doctors had just rang her with the results of the x-ray. A shadow could be seen on her left lung and they were referring her to see a lung specialist. I hugged her and we both cried and I mean we cried lots; we were frightened and felt sick. I had to ring work and tell them I couldn't come in, I had to be with Sharon.

We now had to wait a week before we could see the specialist. Seven days which seemed to last forever. In that week, we tried to carry on as if everything was ok, when really it wasn't. We searched online and read that radiotherapy to the breast can sometimes show up as scarring on the lung. I was even thinking to myself that perhaps there had been a speck of dirt or dust on the x-ray machine, which had showed up as a shadow. It's weird how the mind works when you are desperately searching for answers.

A week later we sat on blue plastic chairs in the hospital, waiting to see the lung specialist. Sharon's name was called and we went into a room, we were both very anxious and nervous but a very small part of us was hopeful, hoping that it was just scarring caused by the radiotherapy.

We both sat down, the consultant looked at us both and said that he was certain that it was the breast cancer that had metastasised, which means that it had spread from the original site to other parts of the body. He showed us the x-ray images and pointed out that there was also another shadow on the other lung. We looked at him, in disbelief and trying to understand it, asked, "So the cancer has come back then?" His response was, that it probably never really went away, the chemotherapy and radiotherapy had helped keep it at bay, but the cancerous

Love Beyond Love

RUSSELL WEBB

LOVE BEYOND LOVE

Russell Webb

BIOGRAPHY & AUTOBIOGRAPHY/ General
BIOGRAPHY & AUTOBIOGRAPHY/ Personal Memoirs

PB £9.99   9781398483729

HB £16.99   9781398483736

EB £3.50   9781398483743

This very personal and moving love story takes us from the anticipation of the very first date through to the moment of the very last breath. It encompasses sheer joy, romance, fortitude and sadness. But love and memories live on forever because this is a Love Beyond Love.

– Jan Smith (a friend)

Please send me ...... copy/ies of

Love Beyond Love

Russell Webb

Please add the following postage per book:
United Kingdom £3.00 / Europe £7.50 /
Rest of World £12.00

Delivery and Payment Details

Format		Price	Qty	Total
Paperback ☐ Hardback ☐				
Subtotal				
Postage				
Total				

Full name: ....

Street Address ....

City:... County:......................................

Postcode: .... Country: ....

Phone number (inc. area code): .... Email: ....

I enclose a cheque for £................. payable to Austin Macauley Publishers LTD.

Please send to: Austin Macauley Publishers Ltd®, 1 Canada Square, Canary Wharf, London, E14 5AA

Tel: +44 (0)20 7038 8212, +44 (0)20 3515 0352

orders@austinmacauley.com
www.austinmacauley.com

AUSTIN MACAULEY PUBLISHERS™
LONDON • CAMBRIDGE • NEW YORK • SHARJAH

cells were already there. We both sat in that room in tears, the consultant was so understanding; he passed us a box of tissues and said he would give us some time to be alone. About ten minutes later he came back in the room and told us what was to happen next.

An appointment was made to see an oncologist, and over the next few weeks Sharon underwent numerous tests and scans, including a brain MRI because by now she was suffering from headaches. Sharon had also noticed a few small lumps appear on her body, one in the centre of her chest about the size of a grain of rice and another of similar size on her face, just above her chin, on the left-hand side.

On 2nd April, we had all Sharon's family over for dinner, it was so nice having everyone there, we laughed and played in the garden. And for that time while everyone was with us it all felt normal, as if nothing else was happening. Once we were on our own in the evening it hit us again like a ton of bricks. By now, Sharon was really in a lot of pain with her back, I bought an electric blanket for her side of the bed, hoping it would help ease the pain.

I am not sure of the exact date that we got the results of the scans, but what I do remember is that we met up with Sharon's children this time, and we all went in to see the oncologist together. I sat next to Sharon holding her hand while her children stood to one side of the room. We were told that the breast cancer had metastasised to her brain, bones, liver, kidneys and skin. We were shown the results of the PET scan which showed the cancer in so many places. The oncologist even commented that he didn't expect to see Sharon looking so well. I'm not going to describe our reactions after hearing the results. All I will say is that it was devastating and we felt numb. I wish I could erase that memory from my mind but I know it will always be there.

Another treatment plan was put in place, which I will talk about later.

We got home that night and we just hugged each other and cried lots. Something I will never forget, was when Sharon looked at our top table wedding flower arrangement, which was now sitting in our lounge on the coffee table, and said that she would like it to be put on the top of her coffin.

Chapter Forty-Nine
A Brave Face

Something that Sharon always did right from the first diagnosis, was to put on her brave face and play things down. She did this to protect her family and friends, when people asked how she was feeling, she would predominately answer with 'I feel fine'. As a parent myself I can understand why she wanted to keep her pain and suffering to herself and not want to worry her children. I have also seen this with my own mum, who for years has suffered with multiple sclerosis, and doesn't say too much to my sisters and me about how she feels. My dad however is with her twenty-four hours a day and it is difficult for my mum to hide her suffering.

Following the appointment with the oncologist the family and myself took time off work to try and make some kind of sense of it all. Being as I have mentioned work, let me tell you about my situation. As you read earlier, I am a full-time fire fighter working for The London Fire Brigade. I do shift work consisting of two 10.5-hour days followed by two 13.5-hour night shifts, then almost four days off duty. So, I was able to spend a lot of time with Sharon and be there for the numerous appointments which we had. Even when the chemotherapy and radiotherapy clashed with my work, I was able to take special leave. My work colleagues and management were very supportive of both Sharon and myself and that support continues today. I think that if I had worked in another job, Monday to Friday 9 to 5, I probably would have been dismissed because I would have been taking a lot of time off. I have always been a hard worker and have never been unemployed, however, with that said, I truly believe that family and loved ones should come first before work.

Sharon wanted to take her children and myself out for lunch and on 10th April we all went to Southend for an afternoon tea and walked along the seafront, following the same route that we took on our very first date.

The lung biopsy was on the next day, 11th April and we had to be at the hospital early. Again, more sitting around in blue plastic chairs waiting for a bed to become free.

The biopsy itself was a difficult procedure, carried out under general anaesthetic, because a long needle enters through the back and into the lung itself to get to the tumour, so that cells can be extracted, for testing in the laboratory.

Whilst Sharon was in the operating theatre, I went into the atrium area of the hospital and sat in the same chairs, in the same coffee shop where we used to meet for lunch. I felt alone and lost, I needed answers to my fears.

Further around the atrium of Broomfield Hospital is a Macmillan Cancer help desk. So, after my coffee I went to see the person at the desk. There were two people there a man and a lady. I asked if they could see me as I had some questions. Now these people were so kind they sat me down behind a green coloured divider for privacy. It was then when I opened up and had tears streaming down my face, I told them of Sharon's diagnosis and that she was currently in theatre. I wanted to know what to expect, I didn't want it to be a shock for me, I wanted to know how she would deteriorate and what I could do to help my wife be comfortable. The Macmillan nurses, I assume they were nurses, were so helpful and compassionate in the way they answered my questions. "Every cancer patient is different and reacts to the disease and the treatment in different ways." I asked again if they could give me some idea as to what may happen to Sharon because of the extent of the metastases. I was told that she could become jaundiced because it was in her liver, and her skin could become itchy. She could become bed ridden and unable to walk. She may also have seizures due to the brain tumours, and could possibly lose weight due to sickness. I am not sure if it's standard practice for them to disclose this information, but they could clearly see I was struggling and I needed to know. Even though what they told me was shocking, I am glad I spoke to them as it prepared me for what could possibly lay ahead.

It was late afternoon by the time Sharon returned from the operating theatre. She was thirsty, hungry and a bit sore, however she still always managed to smile. I didn't tell her that I had spoken with the Macmillan nurses and I never did.

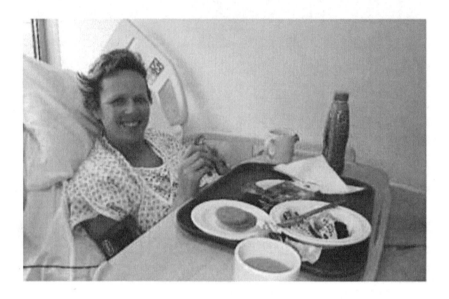

The following day the 12th, we had another family gathering, this time in Southwold, Suffolk. This time all Sharon's family except for her brother were there. We braced the cold wind blowing off the North Sea and walked down the traditional pier. Later in the evening we all had a meal in a lovely restaurant. We had the opportunity to stay the night in a guest house, but we chose to go back home because the next day we had an appointment at the Radiotherapy Centre.

Chapter Fifty
No Cure

The oncologist had told us at the start that there was no cure, but there was treatment available which would help.

When Sharon was first diagnosed with breast cancer in 2016, she was given the choice whether to have treatment or not. I remember her clearly saying that she wanted them to do everything that could medically be done which would help her. The same applied this time, Sharon wanted to live, and by accepting the treatment it could prolong her life. So, a treatment plan was put into place:

Sharon had already been prescribed a high dose of steroids and had been taking them since the appointment with the oncologist. Because of the size and number of tumours within Sharon's brain, the priority was to give a course of targeted radiotherapy to her whole brain. On 13 April 2018, we had an appointment at the Radiotherapy Centre at Colchester Hospital, Essex. This appointment was for Sharon to have a plastic mask made. This process was very distressing to watch and I had to control my emotions. Sharon had to lay completely still on a hard surface, a plastic mesh sheet was then placed in hot water to soften it. Next, the sheet was stretched over my wife's face/head and pulled tight and anchored down. A cut-out was made for her nose to poke through. Sharon had to stay there for fifteen minutes while it hardened. This was to be the mask that she would have to wear whilst they did the radiotherapy. Each time she would be laying still and the mask anchored in place. Sharon was totally calm whilst the mask was being made and didn't complain once. Such a brave woman indeed. Like I said, it was me who had to hold back my tears. Once the mask was made, we were allowed to have a break. Sharon then had to have a CT scan so they could mark the exact locations to be treated.

The radiotherapy treatment on Sharon's brain began on Monday 16 April 2018 and continued every day for a total of ten days, excluding the weekend, with the last session being on Friday 27th April. There were further sessions during May to target other areas, with the main cause for concern being the lump in the middle of her chest, which was now the size of a golf ball. They needed to treat this urgently, because they were concerned that it may erupt through the skin. Thankfully, after five days of radiotherapy it almost disappeared. One time I was asked to circle with a pen every lump that Sharon and I had found on her body for the oncologist to see. There must have been in excess of twenty black circles drawn on Sharon's body.

Chemotherapy began on Wednesday 23 May 2018, and was to continue every Wednesday apart from one. In other words, three sessions out of four. This pattern carried on with no end date scheduled.

As well as the steroids, Sharon had to take so many other tablets. I know this because once again, weekly, I would replenish the tablet box. Sharon had to carry this with her if we went out, as she had to take the drugs at regular times and intervals. She was also prescribed oral morphine as a pain relief, and would generally take it at night, but I do remember times when she had to take it during the day as the pain was unbearable.

Apart from the medical treatment, Sharon had massage treatments at Farleigh Hospice and also at the Helen Rollason Cancer Charity Centre. I also had a couple of massages and reflexology. This really helped to relax us, and for a while we felt 'normal' again, with no stresses or worries.

The first month after receiving the diagnosis; life at home was very difficult at times. Having to adjust again to the numerous hospital and clinic appointments, the taking of medication, and just trying to understand everything; really messed with our heads. Bed time was hard, Sharon would be in a lot of pain and discomfort until the morphine kicked in, and it took her ages to fall asleep. It was during this time that Sharon wanted me to tell her stories to help take her mind off things. This was when I invented 'The Adventures of Little Sharon and Little Russ'. Every night, whilst stroking her face I would softly tell her a story, each time 'Little Sharon and Little Russ' would be going on a different adventure.

Eventually Sharon would settle down and drift off to sleep. I would lay awake for hours, listening to her breathing and would open the curtains slightly to let in the moon-light, so I could see her. I must have had about two hours sleep each night, and the first thing I did when I woke up was put my left arm out to feel her, to see if she was still alive.

On 21 April 2018, the wedding photographer hand delivered our wedding album. Such beautiful photos of a perfect day, we sat in the lounge looking through it together and I took a selfie.

The album has a thick glass front and is too nice to be stored away in a box, so, I made an oak stand for it to sit on, and it was placed on the coffee table next to the wedding flowers. I often look at our album and think about our special day. I also have the photos digitally stored on my laptop and on my phone, as well as on a memory stick, but there is something special about sitting quietly with the album on my lap and turning the same pages that Sharon once turned.

One morning, 26 April 2018 to be precise, Sharon woke up and looked straight at me and said I want to do everything I can to beat this, and I am positive and focussed.

She even sent a message to the family chat group and this is a screenshot of my wife's words.

> **26 APRIL 2018**
>
> SHARON Webb
> Morning family, just wanted to say hi and say I've had a Eureka moment !!! I woke up this morning and was ' do you know what, I will, with the help of my amazing kids and husband do EVERYTHING I can to beat this thing(I'm not in denial lol) I am feeling so strong and super positive (my favourite word)
> off to radio now
> love you all so much and have a great day xxx
> 08:25

From that moment, things changed; I saw the same strong woman that I had seen the year before. Her outlook on life became focussed and positive again. Obviously, the pain and disease were still there but mentally we became stronger.

You already know how much we liked to plan, well, we began to plan days out and weekends away. Sharon booked up meals in nice restaurants well in advance. We planned a holiday in Devon with the family and we booked up for a week's holiday in a cottage in Cornwall just for the two of us. We had to fit these things around the treatment plan, but you know something; having other things to look forward to, kept us focussed on living and really helped. Even on trips to the radiotherapy centre we would make a day of it by going out afterwards, to the beach or for a picnic in a park. We were focussed on doing the things we loved to do rather than just focussed on the cancer and treatment.

Sadly, there were other plans that we had to make and speak about. This being writing our Wills and funeral plans. We both agreed that we would want to be cremated and our ashes interred into a plot at the local cemetery. Sharon wanted this to be a place where family and friends could visit and pay their respects. We made an appointment at the local funeral directors, but when the time came to go there, Sharon was upset and asked if I would go alone. So, there I was sitting in the funeral directors, less than four months after getting married, talking about my wife's funeral. I came out of that office and just broke down in tears, and had to go for a walk to clear my head before going home. I had been given some leaflets with prices which I showed Sharon. We spoke about things for some time and Sharon then asked me, that when the time came, would I mind sorting her funeral out and all the other formalities that needed to be done. She wanted to protect her children from having to do this as it would be really hard for them, they would be going through enough pain without having to worry about anything else. I promised my wife, that I would do this for her. After this conversation, we put the leaflets in the drawer and tried to forget about it. In fact, we never discussed it again, there was no need to. I knew what Sharon's wishes were and what we both wanted and what I had to do.

Chapter Fifty-One
My 'Last' Birthday

Sharon had been planning to take me away to Barcelona for my birthday as a surprise, but following the diagnosis, and being told that she couldn't fly on an airplane put a hold to her plans.

Instead, Sharon surprised me with a lovely trip to the Lake District.

Sharon's last radiotherapy to her brain was on 27 April, the day before my birthday.

This was taken in the same spot where Sharon jumped for joy on 4 July 2017, having competed radiotherapy to her breast.

The car was already packed with our fridge, cooker and flask full of hot water and our journey began as soon as we left the hospital car park.

To break the journey up we had planned to stay overnight in a bed and breakfast. It was a Friday and there was a lot of traffic on the roads, and it took longer than I had anticipated to get there. It was quite uncomfortable for Sharon, her back and legs were aching and even though I had put pillows and cushions around her for support, she still had to take the morphine.

We finally arrived at the B&B, we had packed plenty of food, so being as we were both shattered, we decided to stay in our room and watch the daylight fade away, whilst eating a chicken salad.

Next day, my birthday, Sharon handed me a lovely birthday card with For My Husband on the front. She had written beautiful meaningful words inside. I will treasure this card along with all the other cards that Sharon gave me.

After breakfast, our journey continued to the Lake District, where we stopped for a picnic at Lake Windemere. In true Sharon and Russ style, we parked in a car park and found an area of grass where we laid out the picnic blanket, set up the camping stove and warmed up a couple of tins of soup and had it with some thick crusty bread followed by fresh fruit and yogurt. After lunch, we walked down to the lake to the area where we had stopped on our first road trip back in March 2015.

The guest house that Sharon had booked for us to stay in was in a village on the edge of the Lake District, which was an ideal location, because we were able to use it as a base to explore the lakes and beautiful countryside. On the night of my birthday, Sharon had booked us in to a nearby restaurant and we had a lovely meal.

You may notice that there is just a jug of water on the table, as you read earlier, I don't drink alcohol. Sharon though used to enjoy a glass of wine with a meal, but sadly due to the amount of medication that she was now taking, she was not allowed.

We stayed for a total of four nights in the guest house and during the days we went out visiting different areas. There was one place that we went to, where we walked across a field to get to a lake, it was a beautiful and secluded spot. I laid the picnic blanket out and we must have spent about three hours there, enjoying the warm sunshine and wonderful scenery. We spoke about all sorts of things, and there were also times when we were just quiet, listening to the birds and the sound of the ripples going over the surface of the water. There was one point when Sharon became tired and put her head in my lap, she fell asleep straight away with me stroking her face. I know the exact location of the lake and where we sat, one day on my travels I shall return there and I won't be alone, because Sharon will certainly be with me; in my heart and in my thoughts.

By now, Sharon's hair was falling out in big clumps caused by the radiotherapy to her brain, and it was becoming difficult for her to wash and put a brush through it. Thinking ahead I had taken my clippers away with us, just in case, and it was on the last day that Sharon asked if I could shave her head.

Now, we had done this before and you would think that this time round it would be easier. Well, it wasn't, it was just as upsetting for us both. Sharon had got a new wig, a shorter and different style from her previous one and she had brought it away with us. Once I had finished shaving her head, Sharon went into the bathroom, showered and then got dressed and put her new wig on. She looked stunning as always and the wig looked perfect and so natural. It made Sharon feel so much better in herself.

This photo I took not long after I had shaved her head.

When I look at this photo, I find it so hard to believe that my beautiful wife was very ill. The more I look into her eyes the closer I get and feel myself being drawn towards her. And that smile, well, it just melts my heart.

Chapter Fifty-Two
Busy Times

When looking back at our diaries for May 2018, they were pretty much full up:

We had appointments at Farleigh Hospice where Sharon was seen by a medical clinician, who was able to review Sharon's pain relief. Sharon had always been one for not wanting to take too many tablets, and just put up with the pain. I remember the clinician saying to Sharon that there was no need for her to suffer with pain. She explained the taking of the different pain relief would really help. Sharon was prescribed the maximum dose of standard over the counter paracetamol, to be taken at regular intervals, she was also prescribed a slow-release morphine tablet. What a difference it made to Sharon, yes, the pain was still there but nowhere near as bad as it was.

It was whilst we were at one of the appointments at Farleigh Hospice that we were told of a local Essex charity called, The David Randall Foundation. Taken from their website this is what they do:

'To support people living in Essex with life limiting illnesses to enjoy life to the full for as long as possible, by helping with GOOD DAYS for them and their families'.

'To provide Scholarships and Inspirational Awards to people who demonstrate exceptional dedication and passion in pursuing their ambitions in sport or music but may be held back by their financial situation'.

We were handed an application form, which we had to fill in and write down things that we would like to do, basically like a 'bucket list'. We took the form home and it sat on the dining table for a day, we just couldn't bring ourselves to fill it in. Next day after breakfast, we spoke about the form and the things Sharon would perhaps like to do. After a while and a few tears, Sharon chose the following:

A hot air balloon flight.

A trip to Leeds Castle in Kent, with possible overnight stay.

A trip to Bath and Longleat Safari Park, with an overnight stay for the both of us and for Sharon's daughter and grandson.

I sent the form off later that day and within a day or so I had a call from the foundation. They were going to book and pay for the things that we had put on the list. All we needed to do was provide suitable dates for when we could go. I shall talk more about our good days in a later chapter.

It was also Sharon's daughters' 30th birthday in May, and she was having a big party. It was very important to Sharon that she would be well enough to go. Thankfully the night came of the party and Sharon was there celebrating her daughter's birthday. It was a great night; all Sharon's family and my family were there. I do remember at one point I had to go outside and get some fresh air because I was feeling very emotional. My sister, Angela, had noticed me and came outside to give me a hug.

The reason why I felt sad, was that earlier in the day, Sharon had asked me to get something from her car which was parked on our drive. Since being told that the breast cancer had metastasised (spread) to her brain, Sharon was told that she could no longer drive. This in itself was another blow for Sharon, she loved her little car, it was the first car that she had ever owned in her name. I went to her car to get whatever it was that Sharon had asked me to get, and there in the footwell was her gym bag. I opened the bag and inside were her little fingerless gloves that she wore whilst training, her gym card membership, earphones, a half-opened pack of chewing gum and a small towel. How could something like this cause me to be so upset? I remember thinking, that the last time she used this was when she was well and getting fit and strong again after the first bout of treatment. As I looked through the contents of that small gym bag, I got choked up; I knew that she would never be well enough again to go to a gym. To this day I still have that gym bag with Sharon's bits inside, just as it was and it hangs in my wardrobe next to her black hiking coat.

I went back to work on 7th May after having time off and leave following the diagnosis. Leaving Sharon was really difficult and I was so worried. I used to call her regularly to make sure she was ok and that she had taken her medication.

The weather in May was really nice, in fact the whole of summer 2018 was warm and sunny. We made the most of our time together by going to the beach and just spending time in our garden.

I mentioned earlier that chemotherapy treatment began on Wednesday 23rd May 2018. It was at the same suite where we had been the year before. Sharon also had to have regular blood tests two days before each session, to make sure that her blood cell count was ok. This involved yet another trip to the hospital each week.

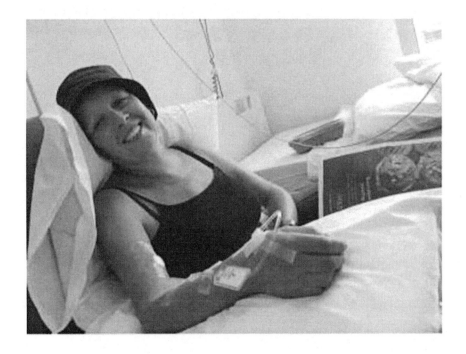

Sharon wanted to have another PICC line fitted but had to wait a week, so the first session of chemotherapy was administered through a vein in her arm. When the time came for Sharon to have the PICC line, the doctor struggled to get the line right the way through, and after some time of trying had to stop.

Sharon was then booked in for 4th June, to have a portacath fitted under general anaesthetic. For those of you who don't know what this is, it's a small chamber that sits under the skin at the top of the chest. Attached to the chamber is a line that sits in a large vein close to the heart. No visible tube can be seen, just a bump where the chamber is beneath the skin. The chemotherapy nurse cleans the area, and with a special needle attaches a drip and the drugs travel from the chamber to the tubing and into the bloodstream. Having the portacath was so much easier for the chemotherapy nurses and was less distressful for Sharon.

On Friday 25th May, Sharon had developed a high temperature and had to go into hospital to have fluids and intravenous antibiotics as a precaution, in case she had an infection. She was back home with me on the Sunday but she was very tired and exhausted.

I fully understand that people may find my words and photos, especially in the last few chapters, upsetting. I am sorry if it offends, but this is the reality of cancer!

To end this chapter on a happier note, remember much earlier when I wrote about concerts and festivals; I said that I would tell you about the last concert that Sharon and I went to:

As you probably have gathered, Sharon was a huge Take That fan. It just so happened that Gary Barlow (the real one) was doing a concert at the Cliffs Pavilion in Southend and as you would expect, the tickets sold out within minutes of coming on sale. A couple of weeks before the concert I emailed the manager of the theatre, explaining that Sharon was terminally ill and was there any chance that we could be squeezed into the theatre. I did get a reply back saying that the concert was fully booked, and to comply with fire regulations they could not fit anyone else in. However, he did say that sometimes they get a cancellation last minute and if this was the case, he would contact me first.

On the morning of 31st May 2018, I had a call to say two tickets were available. I bought the tickets there and then and you should have seen Sharon's face when I told her where we were going that evening.

We dressed up and left home early to miss the traffic and had a meal in a restaurant near to the Cliffs Pavilion.

Once in the theatre we found our seats, we were centre stage about six rows from the front. Not that we sat down much; as soon as Gary Barlow came on stage everyone stood up and danced. The whole night was fantastic, and to see Sharon singing and dancing made me feel so happy. I am so glad that I emailed the manager and so lucky that the tickets became available.

Chapter Fifty-Three
Summer to Remember

So, the summer of 2018 came, and unusually the weather was really nice, hot days with lots of sunshine, which I'm glad about because we spent a lot of time in our garden. I made sure that there was plenty of shade by putting up the sun canopy and had a fan blowing on Sharon to keep her cool in the heat. Along each side of the garden fence, I had put solar fairy lights up, which made our garden look so magical as darkness fell. We would lay on our king size inflatable camping mattress and star gaze, a warm fleece blanket covered us and scented candles flickered in the breeze. Sharon would lay with her head on my chest and my left arm wrapped around her as we looked up at the stars and constellations. Sometimes we would talk about all sorts of things, there were other times when we were quiet and just stared into the night sky. There were also times when Sharon fell asleep in my arms, and I would lay there, listening to her breathing.

In the second week of June, we had a week in Devon with Sharon's family and stayed in a bungalow at The Firefighters Charity Centre, Harcombe House. It was a lovely week having all Sharon's children and grandchildren with us. Sharon was determined that she wanted to do this and I'm grateful to the charity for the help and support they gave us, and continue to give me.

There are many significant dates that I have in my memory, dates when certain things happen, good things and bad things. But one date which is special to me is the summer solstice, 21st June 2018, a truly lovely memory:

The Essex based charity, The David Randall Foundation, which I wrote about earlier, had arranged and paid for us to stay overnight within the grounds of Leeds Castle and for us to have a three-course meal in the restaurant, which overlooked the beautiful castle.

We arrived at the castle around midday and checked into our room which was stunning, white panelled fitted wardrobes went from one side of the room to the other. Taking centre stage was a large white four-poster bed, which had so many pillows on it that I lost count. A dressing table with a selection of teas and coffees and posh mineral water in glass bottles, stood in the corner.

After we made ourselves a cuppa, we went to explore the castle and the other attractions within the grounds. We even went punting on the moat which surrounds the castle.

Whilst walking around the many rooms and banqueting hall within the castle, we felt like a King and Queen; like we had stepped back in time. We must have spent an hour and a half inside looking at the displays and taking photos.

Back in the grounds, we were able to catch the last birds of prey display before making our way to the famous maze and grotto. We had lots of fun here, and I must say that Sharon negotiated the maze just perfectly, leaving me behind, lost within the tall hedgerows.

I would definitely recommend going to visit Leeds Castle and its grounds. The gardens are beautifully kept and there is so much to see and do.

We went back to our room and showered and got changed for our evening meal. Our table in the restaurant, which overlooked the castle, was set up with the seating opposite each other. Without even thinking about it we moved the cutlery and chairs so that we were sitting next to each other.

The meal was really lovely, and we finished dessert just in time to go outside on the terrace with a coffee, to watch the sun set over the castle on the longest day. It really was a perfect moment.

We went back to our room and four-poster bed around 22.30hrs.

Leeds Castle and that date of 21st June 2018 will always be special to me. We had such a wonderful day and evening, and it was also the last time that Sharon and I made love. I will never forget that moment when Sharon came out of the bathroom wearing her bridal underwear. She looked so stunning, just as she did on our wedding night. We hugged each other and kissed, we both had tears in our eyes. It was such an emotional moment.

Next day after breakfast we decided to have another look inside the castle, and Sharon picked out a Christmas Tree bauble from the gift shop. The sad thing is that she never got to see it hanging on our Christmas tree.

Back in the grounds Sharon's energy levels had dropped, and she felt very fatigued and just wanted to lay down and close her eyes. We found an area next to a narrow stream where I put my jacket on the grass and Sharon laid down, with her head resting on my lap, I stroked the side of her face and she fell asleep almost straight away. She must have been asleep for over an hour and I remember seeing two women walk near us. They were close enough for me to hear them say, "Look at her over there, she must have had too much to drink." They were making fun of Sharon. I'm glad that she was sleeping and didn't hear but it really upset me, how dare these two middle aged women judge someone they don't even know. I didn't react to them as didn't want to make a scene and wake Sharon up. A year later on 21st June 2019, I went back to Leeds Castle and spent the day there doing the things that Sharon and I had done. It was very emotional and although I was there alone, I could definitely feel Sharon with me, and she even helped guide me through the maze where I had got lost the year before. My intentions are to revisit the castle and grounds every year on 21st June. Unfortunately, 2020 was a very difficult year with the covid-19 pandemic and the country being put into lockdown, I was unable to go. I'm hoping in future years it shall be open and I will be able to go back to that special place. I didn't stay the night but I did go to the restaurant and sat at the same table. Whilst I was there, I wrote a poem which I posted on Facebook and you can read it here:**(For Sharon Webb by Russell Webb at Leeds Castle).**

A year has gone since we walked hand in hand. Through that stone archway I now walk alone, to where a castle stands all on its own.

Stepping through the tiny oak doorway, looking like a giant, yet today I feel so small. Or is it just the vast banqueting hall?

A moat surrounds me; reflecting light shimmering on ceilings so tall, to be watched by all, or maybe it's only just for me to see.

Back into the grounds; where knights in shining armour once stood, and onto the freshly cut grass; I wonder if I really should.

Into the maze I stroll, a true example of how I feel

225

today…A lost soul with nowhere to go. Down the steps into the dampness of the grotto, with eyes wide open, I stare. It's where we once laughed but now all I can do is share.

As evening falls and guests go home, yet again I feel all alone. A meal awaits me, a table set for two! Oh, Sharon I am so missing you. Couples talking and holding hands, laughing and smiling; it's ok, I'll just sit and carry-on writing.

Clouds begin to cover the sky and I won't see the sunset tonight. In a way, I'm glad because that memory belongs to us; on our special night.

I shall stay until it's time to go; with all our loving memories that I will never let go.

Because the cancer was also in Sharon's bones, her oncologist was concerned that her bones were weakening, and prescribed a bone strengthening drug which was given whilst she was having chemotherapy. We were also told that wherever possible Sharon should use a wheel chair and walking aids, to prevent the risk of any fractures. I borrowed my mum's mobility scooter and we hired a wheelchair from the local Red Cross. I can tell you now, Sharon hated both of these, she was so independent and wanted to walk. So, she bought herself a pretty pink flowered fold-up walking stick, which she kept in her handbag, and would use it if she felt unstable and needed extra support. However, there were times when she was so physically exhausted and fatigued that she would use the wheelchair. One of those occasions was when we went to Longleat Safari Park.

The David Randall Foundation had kindly arranged and paid for Sharon's daughter, grandson and ourselves to stay in a bed and breakfast for two nights, with entrance into the Safari Park. It was the same B&B where Sharon and I had stayed in July 2015, and we even had the same room. Her daughter and grandson had a room next to ours. I didn't say anything, but I felt quite sad being in the same room. It was in that room that I booked the New York trip. At that time, Sharon was well and we had a lifetime ahead of us. At Longleat Safari Park, you drive your car around the enclosures but there is also a part where you park up and walk. It was here that Sharon needed the wheelchair, but insisted on standing for any photos that I took. Next day we visited Bath and again due to the cobbles and uneven pavements, plus the busy streets, we thought it safer for Sharon to use the wheelchair.

Our last holiday to Cornwall began on Friday 6 July 2018, where we were staying in a converted barn on a farm, with stunning views of St Ives Bay in the distance. The weather for the whole week was sunny and hot, which Sharon found uncomfortable at times. By now, she was very fatigued, spending a lot of time in bed. So, we would venture out in the late afternoon, which worked well for us because the temperature was cooling down.

As you read my words, you will observe that I have written 'last holiday' and I have also mentioned the word 'last' in earlier chapters. Yes, they were the last times that Sharon was physically here, but I can tell you now that my wife remains with me always, wherever I go; holidays, birthdays, coffee shops, etc. I feel her with me, guiding me and loving me just as she did when she was here in life.

We spent our time in Cornwall visiting beautiful villages and beaches. There were times that we would sit on the golden sand and have a picnic, Sharon would sit in the shade under a parasol or umbrella. Like I said, she was very fatigued and there were times when she just needed to lay down and sleep. This was when our beach shelter came in very handy.

You know something; even though Sharon was very poorly and fatigued, she still wanted to do things and enjoy life. A fine example of this was the time that we had a go in the cheap inflatable kayak, that I had bought just before we went away. Sharon was nervous about the whole idea and I had to make sure that I packed the flotation devices. With that said, it was fun, I made Sharon a hat out of a knotted hanky, to protect her head from the sun.

There was one evening that we drove to Land's End, we parked the car and we walked down to the famous sign. I asked a passer-by to take a photo of us, sadly it didn't come out too well as it was dusk, and the gentleman wasn't sure how to use the zoom function on my phone camera. All the same I have included it on the next page. I haven't been back to Cornwall since Sharon's passing, but I intend to and I will stand next to that sign, thinking of my lovely wife and our holiday in 2018; and she will be there with me again.

We stayed for a while and watched the sun set whilst sitting on a bench having a drink. It was one of those moments where we just sat holding hands. We didn't have to talk; we knew exactly what each other was thinking.

Near to the Barn conversion, where we were staying, was a car park on a cliff top overlooking the beach below. We spent many evenings here; we didn't go down the steep steps to the beach because it would have been difficult for Sharon to get back up. Instead, we would sit in our camping chairs with a flask of tea and pack of 'healthy' biscuits and watch the sun set. Again, this is another special place that I will never forget. I took many photos here of the sun disappearing behind the gentle waves. There was one particular photo that is special to me and you will see it and read about it in the next chapter.

There was one afternoon that we went into St Ives, Sharon was feeling weak, so she sat in the wheelchair and I pushed her around the bay and in and out of a variety of shops. I can now appreciate how hard and difficult it is for wheelchair users and for the people who push them. Sharon didn't weigh much and I am reasonably strong, but I found it hard work pushing the wheelchair up and down the hills and slopes and across the cobbled streets. We found a quaint little pub overlooking the harbour, where we sat outside with a drink. Even though Sharon had to use the wheelchair at times, we still managed to hold hands whenever we could; having that physical contact was so important for us.

Chapter Fifty-Four
A Glimmer of Hope

We were told that the cancer had spread, there was no cure and all they could do was treat it.

However, we had read about a treatment called immunotherapy, which is a type of treatment that helps your immune system fight cancer. Obviously, my description is very basic; so, I would suggest that you search the internet, to get a better understanding of it.

The treatment though, was still in trial stages and had not been approved in the UK. Sharon was willing to take part in any trials, but unfortunately at the time there were none taking place; however, the treatment was available in other countries, but would be at a cost.

As a family we began to look at the possibility of Sharon having the treatment abroad, we researched various clinics and made contact with them. We spoke about setting up some sort of online crowd funding. It was whilst we were in Cornwall and whilst Sharon was sleeping due to being fatigued, that I sat on the balcony of the converted barn and began to draft a crowd funding page, and think about other ways that we could raise funds to help with the costs.

It was when we got back from our holiday that Sharon and I discussed the crowd funding page and made various changes. We spoke with the family about other ways that funds could be raised. Everyone was willing to do something, Sharon's eldest son was in training to do an 'Iron Man' sporting endurance event. Her daughter and other son were thinking of arranging a music event with local bands at a nearby pub. Even Sharon's grandson was planning on doing a sponsored walk and bike ride. My sister, and her husband were going to arrange a charity football tournament.

After various discussions with the family, Sharon and I agreed that the crowd funding page should go live and it was on 27 July 2018 when it opened, under the title of *Sharon's Fight for Life.*

I mentioned in the last chapter about a certain photo which is special to me, which I took of the sunset whilst we were on our last holiday in Cornwall. Sharon and I were sitting in front of our car, on our camping chairs overlooking the sea, and watching the sun set. Just as I took the photo, some sea gulls gracefully flew into the shot. We both loved the photo and when we got home, I had it enlarged and made into a canvas and placed it on the wall of our dining room. We chose that photo as the backdrop for the fund-raising campaign page.

The photo not only brings back memories of our holiday, but it is also a symbol of strength, determination and everlasting love.

I had the crowd funding page linked to my Facebook page and came up with the idea of asking friends to use the photo as their cover picture; another way of sharing our story and reaching out. Many friends and friends of friends did exactly that, and it wasn't long before there was a constant orange and yellow glow all over Facebook.

With Sharon's help, I designed a leaflet showing our story, with links to the crowd funding page. I got 2000 copies printed and began to post them in every house in the surrounding area of where we lived. There was also a music festival happening in the nearby Hylands Park, so I got some collection boxes and went and stood outside the main entrance, and with the help of Sharon's sister-in-law from her first marriage, we handed out the leaflets. Sharon's son and his girlfriend joined us later in the day. By standing there for a few hours in the morning and the afternoon, we managed to hand out many leaflets and collected in excess of £800 from the kind festival goers.

The online crowd funding was going really well; friends as well as total strangers had read the page and had donated or left kind messages of support and love. I can't thank those kind people enough, it really helped us to stay positive and gave us that hope. Sharon wrote a thank you and you can see the screenshot of that on the next page.

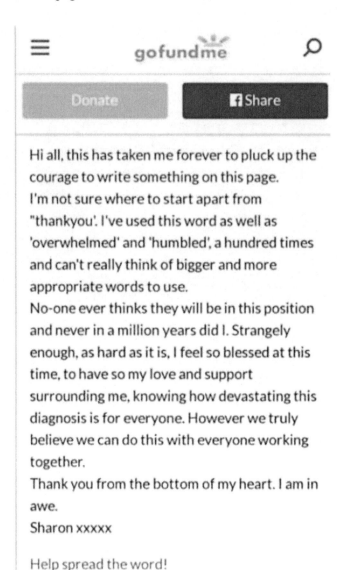

I emailed other fire and rescue services in the UK as well as The New York Fire Department in the USA, asking if they could help. The more people got to read about the campaign, the more the word would be spread. I even wrote to the US President asking for help and support and did get a reply from the White House, saying that they had received my letter and that it was being passed on.

The radio station, BBC Essex, made contact with me and discussed doing an interview on the radio.

The local newspaper and online news contacted us and we were interviewed at home, and our story appeared in the Essex Chronicle on Thursday 9 August 2018.

Whilst I was desperately thinking of ways to raise funds, I was still taking care of Sharon, going to chemotherapy and numerous other hospital and clinic appointments.

By now, Sharon was very weak and had lost her confidence in walking, to help with this she was having physiotherapy at Farleigh Hospice. I sat in a blue chair watching my once fit, strong and healthy wife struggle to walk a few steps with a walking stick and turn around and come back. It was so heart breaking to watch; holding back my tears all I could do was encourage her.

Sharon's eldest son was busy emailing an immunotherapy clinic in Germany and was in the process of obtaining Sharon's medical records from the NHS, so that they could be reviewed by the consultants at the clinic.

Sadly, Sharon didn't get to have any immunotherapy treatment.

After my wife's death, it was agreed between the children and myself that all funds raised would be split three ways, between The Firefighters Charity, Farleigh Hospice and The David Randall Foundation.

Chapter Fifty-Five
The Last Month

There have been parts of this book that I have really enjoyed writing about, such as reliving those beautiful memories of when we first met, our cruise and our wedding.

This chapter though, is one that I have not been looking forward to writing and to be honest I wasn't sure how to tackle it. Should I smooth over the bad parts or do I say how it actually was? I think my best option is to speak from my heart as I have done from the very beginning of this book, but I will however warn you again; you may find my words upsetting. I make no apologies because just like I mentioned before; this is the reality of cancer.

I had begun to notice that Sharon was becoming confused and forgetful at times. The doctors had recently changed the steroids that she was taking, and after reading the small printed piece of paper within the box, one of the side effects was confusion. I telephoned the clinician at the hospice about the change in Sharon and asked if it could be the steroids. Her reply was that it could be side effects, but it was more than likely the progression of the brain metastases. I didn't tell Sharon what had been said, all I said was it is possibly the steroids and that we should mention it to the oncologist at our next appointment.

We had been given a gift voucher for a meal at a Jamie Oliver restaurant, which we had booked for 8 August 2018. In true Sharon and Russ style, we decided to make a day of it, so we also booked to go to the cinema after the meal. The day came and we headed off to Bluewater shopping centre in Kent. Sharon was adamant that she didn't want to be pushed in the wheelchair; she had her fold-up walking stick in her bag just in case she needed it. Together we slowly walked around the centre, I held her hand and supported her all the time. Unfortunately, Sharon had lost her appetite and only ate a small amount of lunch.

The film that we went to see was 'Mamma Mia! Here we Go Again'. I was expecting Sharon to fall asleep whilst the film was showing, but instead she really enjoyed it as did I. It was a fun movie to see, but there was one point where I got choked up and had tears in my eyes, which I managed to conceal within the darkness of the cinema. It was the scene where they sing *'My Love, My Life'*. Nowadays, whenever I hear an Abba song on the radio, I think of that day.

I was still working, doing shifts at the fire station and was becoming more and more anxious about leaving Sharon alone; day times weren't too bad because family and friends would try and call in to see her. It was when I was on night shifts that I really worried. Before I went to work, I would make sure that Sharon had taken the tea time medication, so that all she had to do was take the bed time ones. I made sure that a plastic drinks bottle was next to the bed. Sharon's bed time routine when I wasn't there, would be to put her phone and anything else in a small pale blue cloth bag, which she put over her shoulder; that way she was able to hold onto both handrails, as she slowly made her way up the stairs. She would call me when she was ready to go up to bed, and I then asked her to call me again once she was in bed and settled. My night shifts finish at 09.30hrs which meant I would get home just after 10.00hrs. Most of the time Sharon would still be in bed, but there were occasions when she was awake and sitting down stairs in the garden having breakfast.

When Sharon started to become weak, I showed her how to come down the stairs in the safest way possible, this was going backwards, keeping low and having four points of contact on the stairs, basically crawling backwards. We are taught a similar method in the fire brigade.

We had an appointment at midday on 21 August 2018, with the clinician at Farleigh Hospice. I was off duty on that day and due to go onto night shift later. The weather was nice, I had been awake early and managed to get the laundry done and out on the washing line to dry.

It was more difficult that morning to wake Sharon up for her medication, she just wanted to sleep. I eventually was able to wake her and help her into the shower. She was so confused; she couldn't remember how to turn the taps on. I washed her with soap and water whilst she stood there holding the safety handrails that I had fixed to the wall a couple of months earlier. Back in the bedroom, I got her dressed which was difficult because she just wanted to lay back down. We got to the top of the stairs, I was going backwards and supporting Sharon in my arms, she didn't quite seem right and it was when we got to the fourth step that my beautiful wife collapsed in my arms. Her eyes rolled, she became unconscious and her breathing was shallow. I immediately took my phone out of my pocket and called the ambulance service. At this point, we were still on the stairs, I was stopping Sharon from sliding down, trying to keep her airway open and speaking to the ambulance service. They asked me to count Sharon's breaths, I was told that help was on its way, and that I had to get her onto a flat surface and perform CPR. I carried Sharon's lifeless body down the stairs and placed her in our hallway, not far from the front door to the street. I searched for a pulse but couldn't find one. All the time the ambulance service stayed on the phone which I had on loud speaker. I have performed CPR on many people in my line of work as a fire fighter, but when it's someone you know and love it's entirely different; I felt scared and every bit of saliva in my mouth had gone, I was pushing hard down on her chest, begging for her to wake up.

It must have been around ten minutes that I was doing CPR, however, it felt like a life time. Sharon suddenly woke up dazed and confused just as the paramedics arrived. Sharon was assessed in the back of the ambulance, and by now she was fully awake and not sure what had happened. I called Sharon's children and asked them to meet us at the hospital. I was able to sit in the ambulance whilst it made its way with blue lights flashing and sirens sounding. Just by coincidence there was an ambulance observer on board who Sharon knew from working with her at the hospital. They were chatting away to each other as if nothing had happened.

In the accident and emergency department, Sharon was rushed to the resuscitation room, and once again I was left in a corridor not knowing what to do. A kind nurse showed me to a relatives' room, where I sat and waited and it wasn't long before I was met by Sharon's children. We were eventually able to see Sharon; she was awake, talking and complaining of a sore chest, obviously caused by the chest compressions that I had done. The doctors in the department did say to me that Sharon had had a cardiac arrest and that I had done well to get her back. Later another doctor, said that Sharon had possibly had a seizure and her heart rate would have been so weak it would have been very difficult to find a pulse. To this day I am uncertain what medically happened to Sharon on our staircase, all I know is that I am so glad that I was at home with her, if I hadn't had been, there was a high chance that she may have been found at the bottom of the stairs.

Later that day Sharon was transferred to a ward and had her own room which overlooked the main entrance to the hospital. The room also had its own private shower and toilet facilities. With the help and assistance of one of Sharon's previous ward managers (my apologies if I have got her job title wrong), I was able to stay in the room with Sharon. A fold up bed with fresh linen was wheeled into the room, and instructions were given to the nurses on the ward to look after me.

For months, I had been the one sorting out the medication and making sure that Sharon had them at the right intervals. Now the nurses were doing this for Sharon, and all of a sudden, I felt redundant from my duties. I do remember someone saying to me that it was now my time to be the husband and not the carer. I thought this was a strange thing to say because I was happy being both, however, looking back now I can sort of understand what they were saying to me. They wanted me to enjoy every last minute with Sharon and not have to worry about medications, this was now their job to do.

Day times in the hospital seemed really busy, Sharon had visits from family and friends which was really nice. At night, I set up my bed next to Sharon's. Before I got into bed, I would lean over to my wife and kiss her, stroke her head and I would tell her stories of 'Little Sharon and Little Russ', until she was sleeping. I would lay there in my temporary bed listening to every breath she took. I was so scared to go to sleep myself, in case I lost her during the night.

This next photo is the very last photo taken of Sharon and me together.

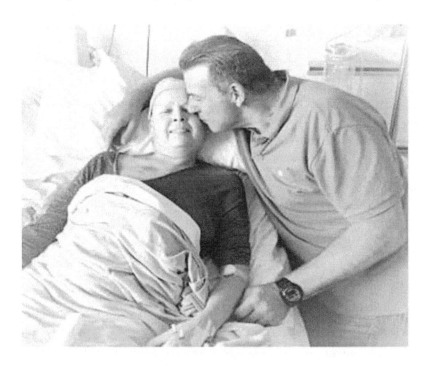

With the help of the hospital and Farleigh Hospice, I was able to get things put in place at home; a special hospital bed with a moving air mattress was delivered along with other mobility aids which would help. Whilst Sharon was being visited by friends on one of the days, I rushed home and removed one of our sofas from the lounge and set up the bed. I made the bed and put our quilt and pillows on it and placed a cuddly teddy bear on it.

Sharon and I remained in hospital for a total of nine nights and on Thursday 30 August 2018, with the help of the hospital and hospice, I was able to carry out Sharon's wish, that being she wanted to be cared for at home. Sharon came home with two syringe drivers, one in each arm. (A syringe driver is a small battery powered pump that delivers medication at a constant rate through a small tube under the skin). All Sharon's medication was now being administered this way.

I remember the drive home in the ambulance. I sat next to Sharon, who was laying down and couldn't see anything, so I described every detail of that journey; our last ever road trip!

That first night back home, Sharon's sister stayed overnight in the spare room, while I carried the mattress from our bed and put it in the lounge next to Sharon. The following nights it was just Sharon and myself. On the Friday and the Saturday, family and friends were in and out most of the day and even though Sharon was very poorly and tired, she was in good spirits. In the early hours of Sunday 2 September 2018, Sharon became agitated and I called her children who came over straight away.

The nurses from Farleigh Hospice, had been calling in to care for Sharon at regular interval during the daytimes. On their first visit on the Sunday morning, they managed to settle Sharon down and make her comfortable.

It was an extremely difficult day for Sharon's children and myself. My sister Angela and my son, Jason, came over in the afternoon to support me. The nurses from the hospice were also there and even stayed beyond their normal finish time; waiting until they were relieved by a Macmillan Cancer Support nurse.

My beautiful wife, Sharon Lynne Webb, fell asleep peacefully at 02.25hrs on Monday, 3 September 2018, with my sister, Angela and my son, Jason and myself at her side.

I phoned Sharon's eldest son, who had left about thirty minutes earlier, and he said he was going to talk to his brother and sister.

The Macmillan nurse was very compassionate and made Sharon comfortable. I had to telephone the out of hours doctors service by using the NHS 111 telephone number, so that a doctor could attend our home to formally pronounce the death. Sadly, no doctor rang me back. The nurse left around 03.30hrs, leaving Angela, Jason and myself in the kitchen and Sharon was laying comfortably and at peace in the bed in our lounge. It must have been around 05.00hrs when my sister went home to her family. At 08.30hrs, I had to telephone my own doctors' surgery to explain that Sharon had died, and that we needed a doctor. Fifteen minutes later my doctor arrived and formally pronounced Sharon's death. I was then able to telephone the funeral directors to arrange for Sharon to be collected.

Sharon's friend, who lived within walking distance of our home, came round just as the doctor was leaving. I hadn't been back in the lounge since Sharon died and it was her friend who asked if she could see Sharon. She went in and I followed, and I am so glad that I did because Sharon looked so beautiful and peaceful, the room was very calm.

The funeral directors came and went into the lounge and put Sharon onto a stretcher. I remember saying to them to make sure that they keep her chemo hat on to keep her head warm. Jason and I stood outside our home watching my wife's body being placed into the back of a black coloured private ambulance. With tears streaming down my face, I asked them to please take care of her. The ambulance drove off down the road and out of sight. Walking back into our home I felt empty, I didn't know what to do. Thankfully, Sharon's friend suggested that she could help to strip the bedding and remove the hospital bed from the lounge. So, this is what the three of us did, we all put the lounge back to what it used to be like.

I cannot thank my sister, Angela and my son, Jason, enough for the help and support they gave to Sharon in her final moments and for being there for me.

If it wasn't for Sharon's friend asking to see Sharon, I probably wouldn't have gone into the lounge again, so I can't thank her enough for giving me that opportunity to see my wife at peace and for her help in getting our lounge back together again.

Chapter Fifty-Six
Special Message

It was on our fourth anniversary of meeting, 8 September 2018, that I found something so special. I had just woken up and needed to find some documents, which I knew were in the bottom of Sharon's wardrobe. As I moved some clothes to one side, I found a cardboard box where I assumed the paperwork was being stored. Lifting the box out, I placed it on the bed and began to look through what was inside.

There I found a box with my name on it, I opened it up to reveal a brand new wrist watch, with a personal message engraved on the back. There was also a small envelope, which had my name on it. I opened it up to reveal a metal card, the size of a credit card…

Wherever you are, whatever you're doing, I'll always be with you I'll love you forever my darling husband Your Sharon XXXX

I sat on the bed in floods of tears. I felt so sad at first and then I began to feel something; like Sharon was sitting next to me on the bed, and all of a sudden, my sadness turned to happiness.

I truly believe that Sharon had wanted me to find this special message and gift on our anniversary, and I believe that she was there in spirit comforting me.

That day I went to Southend and sat on Sharon and Russell's bench, which you read about in an earlier chapter.

The card is in my wallet which stays with me always and I wear the watch on special occasions. I'm too worried that I will lose it or damage it, if I was to wear it all the time.

The photo on the card was taken when we were on our cruise in the Caribbean. I had never seen this photo before until I found it on the card. It was taken with Sharon's phone.

I chose it as the cover photo for this book because Sharon had chosen it for the card. Every time I open my wallet, I see it and think of my lovely wife, and that wonderful cruise. Sometimes I smile to myself and wonder, is she keeping an eye on what I spend each time I open my wallet!

I also believe that Sharon is with me, just like she says;

"Wherever you are, whatever you're doing, I'll always be with you. I'll love you forever my darling husband.
Your Sharon XXXX"

Chapter Fifty-Seven
Loved by Many

In my head, all I could hear was Sharon's voice and the conversation that we had, when she asked me to organise her funeral and to deal with the formalities.

So, this is what I did; I just went into 'auto-pilot' mode, and began the process of notifying the various authorities. I had a list of things to do, which I had written down so that I didn't miss anything. The weeks following Sharon's death were filled with various appointments and phone calls; I didn't have time to grieve, I had a job to do, I had to carry out my wife's wishes; she didn't want her children to have to do anything and was protecting them in their grief. I feel proud that I was able to do this for Sharon and her children.

I went to see Sharon three times whilst she lay in the Chapel of Rest. She looked so beautiful and at peace. The last day that I was able to see her was the day before the funeral. I sat with her for over an hour holding her hand and soon, the warmth from my own hand transferred to Sharon's which felt so wonderful; as if she was holding my hand. I spoke to her and thanked her for loving me and giving me that special gift of love. Before I left the room, I placed a single red rose in her hand and a photo of me, the one that she loved so much, which was the very first photo that she saw of me; my profile photo which I had on the online dating site when we first met.

The funeral of my wife took place on Tuesday 25 September 2018. The amount of people who turned up to pay their respects was a true testament of how much Sharon was loved.

I arranged for the same violinist that we had on our wedding day to play *Can't Help Falling in Love with You,* as I helped to carry my wife's coffin into the chapel. During the service, a song was played through the speaker system within the Chapel. This was *A Million Dreams* from the film 'The Greatest Showman'. Sharon had been to see the film with her daughter and really enjoyed it and loved the soundtrack. At the end of the service, the violinist played, *"All You Need is Love";* the same song that we walked down the aisle to, together as husband and wife, just 263 days earlier.

The wake was held in a huge purpose-built events marquee next to Hylands House. An elegant white painted villa dating back to 1730 which stands within the beautiful Hylands Park Estate in Writtle, not far from where we lived. Sharon and I used to enjoy walking around the park and loved to sample the delicious cakes at the tea room.

Back in May 2018, Sharon's friend came to see her and gave her a small hand-painted terracotta pot, containing a small sunflower shoot, just beginning its journey. We had strict instructions about watering it and repotting it as it grew bigger, but most of all we were told to enjoy it. As I said earlier, Sharon's last summer was really hot and we spent most of our time in the garden, it was such a pleasure watching the sunflower grow tall and strong.

On the day before Sharon died, my sister Angela, went into our garden and cut down the now wilting sunflower head, and retained all the new seeds.

At the wake, Angela handed out small envelopes of seeds, which came from Sharon's sunflower. Also, in the wicker basket containing the small envelopes were some A4 size paper sheets with some words that Angela had written, which were placed on the tables for everyone to read. These are the words from that special tribute:

SUNFLOWERS FOR SHARON

The name sunflower comes from the fact that these flowers grow tall, and always manage to find the sunshine...Something which seemed to happen often on the many trips and adventures that Sharon and Russell went on. Something that we would often laugh about. no matter the season, or location they always seemed to find the sunshine or maybe the sunshine found them?

The seeds in these envelopes came from just one sunflower head. This sunflower was given to Sharon by one of her oldest and dearest friends.

The sunflower head was taken from the garden the day before Sharon passed away.

That day, it was overwhelming to see and feel the amount of support and love which filled and still fills every room in the house.

We hope that when you sow these seeds and they begin to grow tall, they too will find the sunshine. Sit back and relax for a while, soak up their beauty, think of Sharon and smile.

It was both a pleasure and a privilege to know Sharon, be it for a day or a life time.

Such a beautiful, kind, genuine and nice person.

To not have her here, by our side in person leaves such sadness, but the impact Sharon makes on us all, on simply being brave, gracious, strong, dignified and full of love is an imprint to be left on all of our hearts forever.

The following summer, I along with many others planted the seeds and watched them grow, and continue to save the new seeds and plant them. It's so wonderful to watch the little green shoots turn into beautiful tall sunflowers, but for me, the most special part is knowing that they originated from Sharon's sunflower.

On the next page is a photo taken in our garden on 13 July 2018 of Sharon's sunflower. Wherever I am, and whenever I see sunflowers, I think of my lovely wife, wishing so much that she was here with me.

As you could imagine, the day of Sharon's funeral and wake was very emotional, yet it was also a wonderful tribute to an amazing woman, that I am so proud to call my wife.

Sharon wanted for her ashes to be interred into a double grave within the local cemetery, so that there was somewhere for family and friends to visit and pay their respects.

On Friday 5 October 2018, I met with family and close friends at the cemetery, I was handed a purple-coloured box containing the ashes. The weather on that day was sunny and warm, unusual for the time of year. I carried my wife's remains from the office to the grave, which was the other side of the cemetery. It felt like I was carrying the weight of the world in my hands for the five or so minutes that it took to reach the plot.

I got down on my knees and gently placed the box into the ground and read out a poem which I had written that morning:

'As You Settle Down to Sleep'
By Russell Webb

As you settle down to sleep, I'm trying so hard not to frown and weep.

Darling, I really miss you so much, I would do anything to feel your touch.

You, my lovely wife, have and will always be the best.

Where do I go from here? I really wonder why I've been put through this test!

Together we became one and that will always be; a bond, a friendship and true love which everybody could see.

My life changed the day I met you.

Thank you for loving me, being my best friend and for being my lovely wife. This pain I'm feeling now, really cuts like a knife.

They say it will get better in years! But for now, I really can't hold back my tears.

Love You so Much and More xxx

With tears streaming down my face and crying uncontrollably, I stood up, and it was then that my dad put his arms out, hugged me and said, "It's ok now Russell, you can cry, let it out." I will never forget that moment when my dad comforted me.

We then went to the Secret Garden Tea room, where I had arranged for food and drinks; during this time the grave diggers and stone masons were filling in the grave and putting the heart shaped headstone in place. Two hours later we all went back to see Sharon's final resting place, and I placed some red roses in the gold-coloured flower pot.

I visit my wife at least once a week and I get great comfort from being there with her. Sometimes I take a packed lunch with me and a flask of coffee or tea. I have my journal with me and I sit in my camping chair writing notes for this book. Since going to the cemetery, I have met some lovely people, who are all going through their own grief.

I do feel sad at times, because Sharon wanted it to be a place where friends and family can visit her and pay their respects: As far as I know, not many people do actually go there to see her. I know it's a personal choice and for some it may be just too difficult for them and I respect that. As for me, I shall continue to see Sharon and tend to her grave until the day that I die, and then my ashes shall be placed next to my wife's...Sharon on the right and me on the left.

Chapter Fifty-Eight
Lost

The weeks and months that followed were very hard, the darkness of winter was setting in, short days and long nights certainly didn't help with how I was feeling.

At Sharon's funeral, I had so many kind people come up to me and offer their help and support, and said that they would be there for me. I received so many lovely sympathy cards saying pretty much the same. Sadly, apart from my own immediate family, who have always been there for me; there were just a few people who checked in on me from time to time, via a txt message or two. I have met up with a couple of Sharon's friends for lunch, which was really nice and we spoke about Sharon, which I found comforting. But generally speaking, those offers of help and support never happened. I have spoken to many widows and widowers since Sharon passed and it seems to be a regular occurrence, with people making false offers of help and support. I don't feel bad about anyone who said they would be there for me but wasn't, because, it must have been so difficult to know what to say to someone who has just lost his wife. Thankfully, when I wasn't seeing my family, they would call me on a daily basis and just knowing that they were there for me was a great help.

At home, I would walk from room to room, searching and hoping to find my Sharon. I kept everything as it was; my wife's slippers were still next to the bed, dressing gown hanging on the door and her clothes hanging in her wardrobe. I wasn't ready to pack things up. Even though our home stopped feeling like a home the day that Sharon died, it was still our home, and in my thoughts, (which were all over the place) I was hoping and thinking that she may just come home.

Daytimes, when I wasn't at work, I tended not to stay in the house much and kept myself busy by visiting Sharon's grave and going to see my mum and dad. I found myself comfort eating, and it wasn't long before my weight started to increase again.

In the evenings, I would sit in silence, listening to every sound; the clock which used to be so quiet now has the loudest of ticks. When the skies were clear I would go into the garden and sit in Sharon's chair and star gaze, hoping to see a sign. There was one time I said out loud, "Darling, I need to know everything is ok and you are well." Just as my words stopped, a shooting star went across the sky. It was probably a coincidence, but I like to think of it as a sign from my lovely wife.

Once in bed, I would lay awake for ages with the curtains open; letting in just enough moonlight to shine on the dressing gown which was hanging on the back of the slightly open bedroom door. The more I stared at it, the more it looked like Sharon standing there; I really wish she had been. Cuddling Sharon's pillow, I would eventually drift off to sleep, but the first thing that I did whenever I woke up was to reach out to my left, searching with my hand; but all that I could find was a cold empty space.

Like I said earlier, I loved our home, when it was our home, but now I felt lost and empty and it stopped feeling like a home the day that Sharon died. Every time I walked up and down the stairs I was reminded of that day when Sharon collapsed in my arms.

Chapter Fifty-Nine
Life's for Living

I needed to have a break, so in November I went on holiday for a week to Turkey. We always made a point of going away for each other's birthdays; so, I decided to be away on Sharon's birthday, the 17th.

At Gatwick airport, I went to the same restaurant and was given the same table where we both sat on the morning of our honeymoon. It was then, that another wave of grief hit me like a tonne of bricks, I couldn't stop crying and had to go to the toilets to compose myself. The flight and transfer were ok, but when I got into the hotel room, which was lovely and had a beautiful sea view, I broke down again. I took a piece of Sharon's clothing with me, sprayed with her favourite perfume and laid it on the bed next to mine, and put a couple of photos on the balcony, so that Sharon could 'see' the view.

Whilst on this holiday, even though I was on my own I didn't feel alone, I could certainly feel Sharon with me. I did a boat trip and went snorkelling and even went on a jeep safari, and all the time I felt Sharon with me having fun and laughing with me. At times, it was very emotional but all in all it was a much-needed break, and I am glad that I went.

Sharon was full of life and wanted to live it to the full, and even though she had received a terminal cancer diagnosis, she still wanted to do things and have things to look forward to. We had many deep conversations and one of those was about me and my future, after her death. She held my hands and looked straight and deep into my tearful eyes and calmly said, "Babe, I want to know that you will be happy again one day, I don't want you to be that lost soul that you were when I met you. I want you to travel to the places that we had planned as well as different places, making new memories. Most of all, I want you to love and to be loved again." Well, I replied with, "I don't want to do anything without you, and as for loving again, well that will never happen." She responded with, "Babe, I love you so much and I will always be with you, wherever you go and I will be there having fun with you. You have my blessing to love and be loved again."

We never spoke about it again, but thinking about it now, it was a wonderful thing for my beautiful wife to say. It must have been so hard for her.

I miss my lovely Sharon so much.

Chapter Sixty
Support

It was about a month after Sharon died, when I started to search the internet for help, advice and support about grieving, that I found a widow and widowers Facebook group. There are lots available, but the one that I joined is based in the UK. I stayed silent at first and just read posts and comments from people who were in the same position as me. Eventually I introduced myself and told them about the loss of my wife. The support and comments that I received have been a great help. Before I found the group, I was beginning to think that it was just me going through so much pain and grief. After reading other widow and widowers' stories, I soon realised that I wasn't alone. This group is full of amazing people, who are all at different stages in their journey.

I have met up with some lovely people from the group, and it's been really helpful; sharing the way we feel and talking about how we get through each day.

We all grieve the loss of our loved ones in different ways; there is no right or wrong way to grieve. When you hear people at funerals and wakes saying 'time will heal', let me just say this; there is certainly no time limit on grief. Time never heals losing someone close; we just learn different ways to cope with the pain. I have spoken with people, who are just weeks into their journey of grief, and have also spoken with people who are years down the line and there is no change, we all still grieve and miss our loved ones, time does not heal that empty space that we have in our hearts.

Whilst I was doing my internet searching, I was drawn towards a book called, *'From Hell to Happiness', by the author Christopher Cooper.* I purchased the book and started to read it just before I went to Turkey. I'm normally a slow reader, but for some reason I managed to finish this book in a few days. The book follows Christopher Cooper and his family through his wife's journey with breast cancer.

As I read his book, at times it was like I had written it myself. Christopher's story gave me the inspiration to write my book; *'Love Beyond Love'.*

Before Sharon died, when we were planning different ways to raise funds for the Sharon's Fight for Life campaign, my good friend, contacted me and offered to arrange a charity showcase evening; featuring a variety of acts with *"Gary Barlow, Take That and the Jersey Boys"* being part of the line-up. It was a great idea and Sharon and I were really looking forward to going. The date was scheduled for November 2018.

I spoke with my friend after Sharon's passing, and she asked if I wanted the showcase evening to go ahead, in the memory of Sharon and to raise funds for the three charities: The Firefighters Charity, The David Randal Foundation and Farleigh Hospice.

On 10 November 2018, exactly three years after I had proposed to Sharon in New York, the Charity Showcase Evening took place. This is my account of that night…

Entering the large hall where tables and chairs are spread around, I can see my family and friends, as well as old friends that I have not seen for a number of years. My eyes are drawn towards the stage, where a slide show of photos of Sharon and myself are being projected onto a large screen. I feel very emotional at this point.

Halfway through the evening I am called up on stage to talk about Sharon and the charities. Thankfully I had prepared something the day before.

For each act that performed, the dance floor was packed, people having fun, singing and dancing. Even though Sharon wasn't physically there in person, I along with others who knew her could definitely feel her presence.

That night I met old friends who never knew Sharon, as well as total strangers, who came up to me and hugged me and shook my hand. Many spoke of Sharon's beautiful heart-warming smile.

Sharon had once again touched the lives of so many, even strangers that didn't know her, went home that night with a smile on their faces.

Chapter Sixty-One
Learning to Cope

The first six months after losing Sharon were very hard. Yes, I went away on holiday which was helpful and I had support from my family and friends, as well as new friends that I had made from the widow/widower's Facebook group. But it was tough trying to adjust to life without Sharon.

Christmas 2018 was fast approaching, and I had offers from my family and friends to go to them for dinner. However, I knew what I wanted to do; I needed to have Christmas dinner with Sharon at the cemetery. So, this is exactly what I did; I cooked a three-course dinner with all the trimmings, then put it in an insulated box to stay hot, and loaded up my car with the garden table and chair. I sat with Sharon and we had dinner together on our first Christmas as husband and wife.

When Sharon was told that there was no cure, she said to me that she had goals to reach, one of those was our first wedding anniversary, 5 January 2019. We had spoken about having a party with live music. Our wedding day was so special; we wanted to celebrate our anniversary and remember that wonderful day.

I was determined to celebrate our anniversary, so, I hired the village hall and booked a musician/singer for the night. I had a projector screen set up with photos of our wedding day and honeymoon continuously playing. On each side of the stage, there was a life size cardboard cut-out of Sharon in her wedding dress and one of the pair of us, taken just as we left the wedding chapel, as husband and wife. Sharon may not have been there in person, but I could definitely feel her presence, singing and dancing and having fun. It was an emotional night but it was also a night for everyone to remember our wonderful wedding and to pay their respects to my beautiful wife.

In March 2019, the rental agreement on my home was due for renewal, and after a lot of thinking and many tears, I decided to find another place that I could call home. It was extremely difficult packing up the contents of our home, I remembered how happy we were when we moved in just a year before. I managed to find a lovely cottage in the countryside with stunning views and Sharon is truly there with me. I have photos on almost every wall, her dressing table stands in the bedroom with her perfume and products in the same place as they were at our home. Sharon's dressing gown is on the inside of the wardrobe. Even though Sharon never knew this new home of mine, I definitely feel her there with me. In fact, I feel her with me always.

Earlier I spoke about the David Randall Foundation and the wonderful things that we were able to do. Well, one thing that Sharon would have loved to do, but sadly never got the chance, was the hot air balloon flight. We did have dates booked, but each time it was cancelled, due to bad weather.

Not long after Sharon died, I contacted the foundation and said that I still had the voucher, and could I return it so that someone else could use it. The lady I spoke to kindly replied, "Take someone else and do it in Sharon's memory."

This is my account of what happened on 21 April 2019 and what I posted on my Facebook page:

In memory of my lovely wife, Sharon Webb:
An early start, I picked my daughter, Mia, up at 04.45hrs. We had to be at the meeting place at 05.30hrs.

It was a beautiful crisp morning. There was a mist sweeping across the meadow, droplets of dew on the grass began glistening as the sun appeared through the trees.

Two balloons were taking off from there that morning. Our one; a multi coloured one, and a bright red one.

A total of sixteen people and one pilot were in our balloon. We all helped to inflate it, opening the massive canopy. Such a graceful and spectacular sight to see fill up.

We slowly and gently began to rise off the ground. Tall trees soon became small as we headed into the clear blue skies over our beautiful Essex countryside.

The whole experience from start to finish was amazing. I am sure that Sharon was there with Mia and myself, enjoying the fantastic views and feeling the breeze on her face.

At the end of the flight, we were handed a certificate and two glasses of champagne. Mia had great pleasure in drinking Sharon's glass.

Chapter Sixty-Two
Special Connection

I had been told that you have to wait six months before you see a medium, I've since found out that you don't have to wait at all. I was always sceptical about mediums and had never had any readings.

It was early April 2019 that I made an appointment to see a medium. First though I did some research and read many reviews. I chose a female medium known as Caressa from Brentwood, Essex, who had many good reviews and people had been back time and time again. When making the appointment, all I gave was my first name.

Sitting with Caressa in her converted summer house, I felt a bit nervous at first, but soon felt relaxed after she explained how the reading would go. Well, to say I was amazed, would be an understatement. The energy and love that I could feel, blew me away. Caressa told me things that only Sharon and I knew about. She spoke of the cruise that we went on, and even said about our plans of doing a Route 66 road trip, and many other things that are personal to Sharon and myself. Readings generally last between forty-five minutes to an hour, however on this occasion, Sharon's energy was so strong it went on for nearly two hours. As I stood up to leave, Caressa said to me, "Would you mind if I hug you?" I said, "Yes Ok, why not?" As soon as she put her arms around me, I felt an energy pass through my body, as though it was Sharon hugging me, which was amazing. From that moment on, I felt totally different, I had connected with Sharon via Caressa and all the way home I just couldn't stop smiling.

I have seen Caressa a few more times since, but I have also seen other mediums, and each time, Sharon has come through and made contact. One medium said about my brother: Remember reading in the early chapters, when I said that for seven years, I thought that I had killed Steven. I never told anyone about this except for Sharon. The medium was talking away and then all of a sudden, the colour drained from her face and she said, "That's why you're here, your wife has just told me that you blamed yourself." With that said, she described Steven perfectly, with his pure blonde hair.

Another medium that I had heard about is Ronnie Buckingham, who has also written a book called *'Medium Rare'*, which I have read. Ronnie has a long waiting list for private readings; however, he does do local theatres and village halls, where he stands in front of a small audience and he receives messages from people who are now in the spirit world. Thankfully, I was able to get to be in one of the audiences and the first person who came through was Sharon. Ronnie described her in detail; saying how she had cancer and that it wasn't just in one place. In the summer of 2020, in between Covid lockdowns, Ronnie rang me and said that he had a cancellation and offered me the chance to have a private reading. Again, it was amazing and it couldn't have come at a better time, which you shall read about in the next chapter.

At the very first meeting with Caressa, she said that I had a strong spiritual awareness and that I had a gift, and I should look into it further. I have read a couple of books about mediumship, but that is as far as I have got. Writing my own book has taken time and been an emotional rollercoaster journey.

With that said, I feel Sharon with me; sometimes I sit on the edge of our bed and it feels like she is sitting right there next to me. I talk to Sharon lots, whether in my thoughts or out loud, this could be anything from a few sentences to a long conversation. I can hear her voice in my mind.

Since my lovely wife has passed, I have been left signs and heard things. A white feather appeared which was stuck to an unopened bottle of Sharon's wine, which had been dusted, just the day before. I found it in the wine rack in a room with no open windows.

Then something really strange happened in the summer of 2019, 30th June to be precise; I was sitting in Colchester hospital with my mum and dad. Dad had an appointment in the x-ray department. The waiting area was very busy yet it was unusually quiet. My mind began to wander to the time less than a year earlier, when Sharon and I sat in the same waiting area; she had fallen over just outside of the hospital and needed to have an x-ray on her cheek bone. Thankfully, there were no fractured bones, just bruising. Just as I was having these thoughts, the silence was broken; a nurse came to the opening and called out the name of the next person to be seen; "Sharon Webb, this way please." Sitting opposite me, a tall, slim woman with blonde hair stood up and followed the nurse. My emotions were all over the place, I felt immense excitement when I heard her name being called, then sudden disappointment when the other woman stood up.

I couldn't see the lady's face; she had her head down and her hair naturally fell forward blocking my view. I wanted to get up and follow her, but it would have been inappropriate. I asked my mum and dad if they had heard the nurse call and they both said no. Mind you, Dad didn't have his hearing aids in and Mum was flicking through a magazine.

Was this a total coincidence or was it a sign from Sharon? I like to think it was definitely a sign.

Chapter Sixty-Three
Mum and Dad

When I began planning and writing this book, I didn't think for one minute that I would have to include this chapter.

It was at the beginning of summer 2019 that my dad started to have some health issues. For the next six months, my dad had many visits to his doctors and had a few stays in hospital with various things, including a couple of incidents where he had fallen over and hurt himself. On one occasion, the ward that he was on overlooked the radiotherapy suite, where Sharon and I had spent a lot of time, and it triggered many memories.

I watched my fit and strong dad, become weaker and weaker, he lost his self-confidence and he was very anxious.

Dad went into hospital on 8 December 2019 with a number of problems, one of those being a very painful back, which made him unable to stand and get off the chair at home. After investigations and tests at the hospital, he was diagnosed with a spinal infection, which needed a long course of antibiotics, administered intravenously. With that in mind, the doctors decided to fit a PICC line. The plan was; Dad was to be allowed to come home and be visited by the district nurse, who would give the medication.

On 23 December 2019 at around 05.00hrs, I was woken up by a phone call from the hospital. A call that I had

been dreading. I picked up my sister Angela, and we got to the hospital just after 06.00hrs.

Dad had already died peacefully in his sleep; two days before his 79th birthday (Christmas Day). I held his hand which was still warm and I kissed him on his head, just like he used to do with me when I was a little boy.

The hardest thing that my sisters and I had to do, was tell our mum that the man she had loved since she was a teenager, had died.

The next five months were very stressful, it was hard to grieve our dad, because we were busy trying to console our mum, putting various care plans in place for her. Mum had suffered with multiple sclerosis for many years and dad had been her carer.

In April 2020, Mum went into hospital with a UTI (urinary tract infection) which was being treated successfully with antibiotics. This was in the height of the pandemic and no-one was allowed to visit her. Sadly, whilst my mum was there, she contracted the covid-19 virus.

In May, Mum was transferred to a care home, not far from where she lived. We were now able to see her, albeit whilst standing outside and looking through the window of the ground floor room.

Our lovely mum passed away on 25 May 2020, just five months after we lost our dad.

Mum and Dad on their wedding day, 7 March 1964.

Our wedding day 5 January 2018

Losing my wife and both my parents in less than two years has been extremely hard. Just when I feel I am coping reasonably well, another wave of grief hits me. Something that I will say, is that the grieving is different; that doesn't mean I miss my mum and dad any less than I do Sharon or vice versa. So many people have said to me how mentally strong I am, and if it had been them, they would have crumbled by now. I'm not going to lie; it has been difficult; however, life is for living and to live it I have to be strong and stay positive. Like I said earlier, there is no time limit on grief. For me, grieving my losses will always be there, but I learn ways to deal with it by making new memories along the journey which I am on.

I think of the time when Sharon was upset because she would not be there to support me when my mum and dad passed. Well, she may not have physically been there, but in spirit she was, and there are times when she channels her energies through the people who are close to me. Sharon continues to love and support me always.

It is now May 2021; it is coming up to a year since I lost my mum and what a year it has been; my sisters and me having to go through our mum and dad's belongings was very emotional, but at the same time it has brought us closer together. We found things which Mum had hidden such as little messages and poems which made us smile. My older sister, Janice, and I found a box of things that had belonged to our brother, Steven. We found toys that I remember playing with and even a pair of leather sandals, scuffed and worn down on one side. The same sandals that he is wearing in the photo on page 22 of this book. Also, we found an audio tape of Steven singing nursery rhymes whilst he was in hospital. To hear Steven again after all those years was amazing. I recorded it on my smart phone and saved it. I often listen to it and think back to my childhood days when I used to play games with my little brother.

To my mum and dad:

Thank you for giving me life and for being the best parents that anyone could ask for. I'm so proud to be your son.

To my brother, Steven:

You are always in my thoughts. You are now with Mummy and Daddy again.

Chapter Sixty-Four
Moving Forward

From those very first messages that we exchanged and our first date, my life as I knew it changed for the better, and I only have one person to thank for showing me how to be loved and how to love, and that is my wife, Sharon. The love between us grew into something so special and wonderful; together we became one.

Sadly, there were people who doubted us and our relationship. Sharon and I didn't let negative comments get in the way; we just carried on loving and used to say to each other, *"We showed them, didn't we?"* Maybe these people were jealous of the love we had, and if that was the reason, then I feel sorry for them.

So, to moving forward; I am now in a new relationship and life for me is improving. Which doesn't mean that I have moved on from Sharon; I have just moved forward with Sharon; she is and will always be in my life and the love will always be there. I will continue to talk about her and share stories of the special times that we had. Even though I am legally not married, (because my wife died), in my eyes, I shall always be married. I still wear my wedding ring and wear Sharon's around my neck, and don't expect that I will ever want to remove them.

My new partner, who I shall name in my next book, is very understanding of the situation and of my needs. She continues to stand by me and support me in my grieving for Sharon and my mum and dad. She has even helped and encouraged me to write this book and is very respectful of Sharon.

Sharon wanted me to be happy again and didn't want me to be that lost soul that I was when she met me. She wanted me to be loved and for me to love again.

I didn't for one minute think that I could find happiness again, but I have, I truly believe that Sharon is looking out for me, and has guided me towards my new partner.

So, to my new partner, who said that she will never read this book, (but I think she will), I want to say to you thank you for being there for me and for picking me up when I have felt down. I look forward to our adventures together and making new memories.

Chapter Sixty-Five
No Ending

I've been asked how I intended to end this book. Well, all love stories generally have an ending, whether that be a sad one, or a happy one. However, me being different, all I will say is this love story has no ending. The love that Sharon and I had will always be there, her memory will live on and she will never be forgotten by those people lucky enough to have been touched by her love, kindness and beautiful smile.

To my lovely wife, Sharon Lynne Webb:

Thank you so much for all the wonderful memories that I will cherish always. Thank you for answering that very first message I sent to you. Thank you darling for loving me and giving me that gift of love. Which shall always be known as a...

LOVE BEYOND LOVE.

I love you, my darling, and always will. Miss you so much and more. XXX
25 September 2021.

Finally...

To you, the people reading my story, I want to say thank you so much. All profit made from the sale of this book will be shared amongst the following charities. Cancer Research UK and the Fire Fighters Charity.

Even though you may not have known Sharon, she has now touched your lives and her strength, courage, determination and love shall live on in you.

Appreciations

Thank you so much to Jan. Smith, who helped to relax Sharon during the many chemotherapy sessions, by doing reflexology. Jan. has also helped me so much with the proof reading of this book and has written the words on the back cover.

To all the staff at Broomfield Hospital and Farleigh Hospice who helped and cared for Sharon. Thank you so much.

Many thanks to my daughter, Mia Webb, who has helped me with the design of the front and back covers.

To all my family: thank you so much for your love and continued support.